PLAYS

Companion Text for College Writing 11.3x

NATHAN TAYLOR

WAYZGOOSE PRESS

CONTENTS

INTRODUCTION

The theatrical play is an immensely important literary art form that has existed for thousands of years. Traversing borders and cultures, from the Ancient Greeks to the Elizabethans, plays have operated as an essential source of entertainment and have been used to critique societal practices as well as reflect on specific times and places. Plays can be imaginative and realistic; comedic and tragic; complicated and simplistic; extravagant and restrained. Like books, the possibilities are endless.

However, there is a major distinction between reading a play and seeing a performance of that same work. A performance is an interpretation made by the actors, director, and others involved in the production. Because every person is unique and possesses a different perspective, as well as dissimilar ideas and personalities, varying emphasis is placed on particular scenes or distinguishing idiosyncrasies of the characters. For example, one might read a sentence and procure a certain connotation from it, while another person might read that same sentence and derive an entirely different understanding. One interpretation is not necessarily more right or wrong than the other, but by emphasizing certain words or phrases, a specific meaning is obtained nonetheless. Similarly, performance focuses the scope of the work to a more particular meaning. By reading a play, however, one is exposed to all of the nuance of the text, and it is left up to the reader to analyze and interpret what he reads.

Reading plays can be difficult, especially if one's exposure to theater has exclusively been the performance aspect. However, plays are meant to be performed, written with the intention that multiple stagings will be produced. Because of the absence of this visual element when reading a play, it can be challenging and even frustrating to imagine the playwright's intended staging or follow the plot or understand the subtleties of what is transpiring on the page. Reading the play aloud can help limit this kind of confusion by bringing the words to life, putting the reader in the position of being all the actors. Finding a group of friends with which to read the play aloud can be even more beneficial because this allows one to distribute the roles amongst other people—helping to distinguish between the numerous characters—rather than reading all of the parts alone, obfuscating any sense of clarity. If coordinating schedules with friends is too complicated, then listening to or watching productions online can be exceptionally constructive. Numerous versions are available for reference, and viewing these stagings or listening to audio recordings can help assist one's knowledge of the text.

In addition, pretending to be the director of the play whilst reading the script can further aid one's comprehension. By imagining all the possibilities for the setting and characters, one can more easily analyze and interpret the larger themes of the work. Being a director is all about visualization; seeing the bigger picture and understanding how everything connects and works together to create the overall desired effect. Putting oneself in the director's chair can be a fun and insightful strategy for making the text more accessible.

Reading the text multiple times is perfectly acceptable. Because the visual component is missing, rereading is occasionally necessary for full comprehension to be achieved. While this strategy is more time-consuming than others, it can be especially rewarding because it gives readers a more rounded understanding of the various characters and a stronger familiarity with the themes and major plot points of the story. If one does not feel confident about his or her understanding of the text after a single read through, there is no need to worry or feel defeated because going through the sections that are particularly difficult to comprehend for a second or even third time will usually resolve this confusion. Patience and determination will make the reading process much easier and less stressful.

William Shakespeare's *A Midsummer Night's Dream* and Edmond Rostand's *Cyrano De Bergerac* are great plays with which to begin implementing these reading and comprehension tactics. Despite the fact that these plays are centuries old, with dense language and a plethora of characters that can be difficult to differentiate, by enacting theses strategies one can have an enlightening and satisfying literary experience and learn something of a different time and place.

A MIDSUMMER NIGHT'S DREAM

William Shakespeare

BACKGROUND TO A MIDSUMMER NIGHT'S DREAM

Arthur Rackham Illustration from A Midsummer
Night's Dream

William Shakespeare is often regarded as one of the greatest writers in the English language. While few historical records survive to explain the details of such a prolific man's life, some facts are known or have been deduced. Born in 1564 in Stratford, England, Shakespeare rose to prominence during the Elizabethan Era as an integral part of the London theater scene. He was a member of the theatrical troupe the Lord Chamberlain's Men—later renamed the King's Men following the death of Queen Elizabeth I and the ascension of King James I to the throne—writing on his own as well as collaborating with other actors, poets, and playwrights in composing at least 37 plays including *King Lear*, *Macbeth*, and *Hamlet*.

A Midsummer Night's Dream is another example of such a play.

Written at the end of the 16th century around the same time Shakespeare would have been creating the famed tragic romance, *Romeo & Juliet*, Shakespeare parodies many of the traditional love stories of his time through his comedic tone and exaggeration of numerous love conventions in Elizabethan society. Furthermore, the incorporation of the play-within-a-play trend at the end of *A Midsummer Night's Dream* mocks the limitations of Elizabethan theatrical customs, heightening the comedic tone for audiences aware of such norms.

In addition to his theatrical work, Shakespeare wrote 154 sonnets along with a number of other poems throughout his career. After years of working in London, Shakespeare retired to his hometown of Stratford where he died on April 23, 1616 at the age of 52. While popular but not particularly revered during his lifetime, Shakespeare has gained a reputation among modern scholars, intellectuals, and educators as a genius, celebrated, performed, and adored internationally. Because of the universality of the themes present in his work, Shakespeare has stood the test of time.

DRAMATIS PERSONAE

THESEUS, Duke of Athens
EGEUS, father to Hermia
LYSANDER, in love with Hermia
DEMETRIUS, in love with Hermia
PHILOSTRATE, Master of the Revels to Theseus
QUINCE, a carpenter
SNUG, a joiner
BOTTOM, a weaver
FLUTE, a bellows-mender
SNOUT, a tinker
STARVELING, a tailor
HIPPOLYTA, Queen of the Amazons, bethrothed to Theseus
HERMIA, daughter to Egeus, in love with Lysander
HELENA, in love with Demetrius
OBERON, King of the Fairies
TITANIA, Queen of the Fairies
PUCK, or ROBIN GOODFELLOW
PEASEBLOSSOM, fairy
COBWEB, fairy
MOTH, fairy

MUSTARDSEED, fairy

PROLOGUE, PYRAMUS, THISBY, WALL, MOONSHINE, LION
are presented by: QUINCE, BOTTOM, FLUTE, SNOUT,
STARVELING, AND SNUG

Other Fairies attending their King and Queen
Attendants on Theseus and Hippolyta

ACT I

SCENE: Athens and a wood near it

ACT I. SCENE I. Athens. The palace of THESEUS

[Enter THESEUS, HIPPOLYTA, PHILOSTRATE, and ATTENDANTS]

THESEUS. Now, fair Hippolyta, our nuptial hour
  Draws on apace; four happy days bring in
  Another moon; but, O, methinks, how slow
  This old moon wanes! She lingers my desires,
  Like to a step-dame or a dowager,
  Long withering out a young man's revenue.

HIPPOLYTA. Four days will quickly steep themselves in night;
  Four nights will quickly dream away the time;
  And then the moon, like to a silver bow
  New-bent in heaven, shall behold the night
  Of our solemnities.

[Exeunt all but LYSANDER and HERMIA]

LYSANDER. How now, my love! Why is your cheek so pale?
    How chance the roses there do fade so fast?

HERMIA. Belike for want of rain, which I could well
    Beteem them from the tempest of my eyes.

LYSANDER. Ay me! for aught that I could ever read,
    Could ever hear by tale or history,
    The course of true love never did run smooth;
    But either it was different in blood-

HERMIA. O cross! too high to be enthrall'd to low.

LYSANDER. Or else misgraffed in respect of years-

HERMIA. O spite! too old to be engag'd to young.

LYSANDER. Or else it stood upon the choice of friends-

HERMIA. O hell! to choose love by another's eyes.

LYSANDER. Or, if there were a sympathy in choice,
    War, death, or sickness, did lay siege to it,
    Making it momentary as a sound,
    Swift as a shadow, short as any dream,
    Brief as the lightning in the collied night
    That, in a spleen, unfolds both heaven and earth,
    And ere a man hath power to say 'Behold!'
    The jaws of darkness do devour it up;
    So quick bright things come to confusion.

HERMIA. If then true lovers have ever cross'd,
    It stands as an edict in destiny.
    Then let us teach our trial patience,

Because it is a customary cross,
As due to love as thoughts and dreams and sighs,
Wishes and tears, poor Fancy's followers.

LYSANDER. A good persuasion; therefore, hear me, Hermia.
I have a widow aunt, a dowager
Of great revenue, and she hath no child-
From Athens is her house remote seven leagues-
And she respects me as her only son.
There, gentle Hermia, may I marry thee;
And to that place the sharp Athenian law
Cannot pursue us. If thou lovest me then,
Steal forth thy father's house to-morrow night;
And in the wood, a league without the town,
Where I did meet thee once with Helena
To do observance to a morn of May,
There will I stay for thee.

HERMIA. My good Lysander!
I swear to thee by Cupid's strongest bow,
By his best arrow, with the golden head,
By the simplicity of Venus' doves,
By that which knitteth souls and prospers loves,
And by that fire which burn'd the Carthage Queen,
When the false Troyan under sail was seen,
By all the vows that ever men have broke,
In number more than ever women spoke,
In that same place thou hast appointed me,
To-morrow truly will I meet with thee.

LYSANDER. Keep promise, love. Look, here comes Helena.

[Enter HELENA]

HERMIA. God speed fair Helena! Whither away?

FLUTE. What is Thisby? A wand'ring knight?

QUINCE. It is the lady that Pyramus must love.

FLUTE. Nay, faith, let not me play a woman; I have a beard coming.

QUINCE. That's all one; you shall play it in a mask, and you may speak as small as you will.

BOTTOM. An I may hide my face, let me play Thisby too. I'll speak in a monstrous little voice: 'Thisne, Thisne!' [Then speaking small] 'Ah Pyramus, my lover dear! Thy Thisby dear, and lady dear!'

QUINCE. No, no, you must play Pyramus; and, Flute, you Thisby.

BOTTOM. Well, proceed.

QUINCE. Robin Starveling, the tailor.

STARVELING. Here, Peter Quince.

QUINCE. Robin Starveling, you must play Thisby's mother. Tom Snout, the tinker.

SNOUT. Here, Peter Quince.

QUINCE. You, Pyramus' father; myself, Thisby's father; Snug, the joiner, you, the lion's part. And, I hope, here is a play fitted.

SNUG. Have you the lion's part written? Pray you, if it be, give it me, for I am slow of study.

QUINCE. You may do it extempore, for it is nothing but roaring.

BOTTOM. Let me play the lion too. I will roar that I will do any man's heart good to hear me; I will roar that I will make the Duke say 'Let him roar again, let him roar again.'

QUINCE. An you should do it too terribly, you would fright the Duchess and the ladies, that they would shriek; and that were enough to hang us all.

ALL. That would hang us, every mother's son.

BOTTOM. I grant you, friends, if you should fright the ladies out of their wits, they would have no more discretion but to hang us; but I will aggravate my voice so, that I will roar you as gently as any sucking dove; I will roar you an 'twere any nightingale.

QUINCE. You can play no part but Pyramus; for Pyramus is a sweet-fac'd man; a proper man, as one shall see in a summer's day; a most lovely gentleman-like man; therefore you must needs play Pyramus.

BOTTOM. Well, I will undertake it. What beard were I best to play it in?

QUINCE. Why, what you will.

BOTTOM. I will discharge it in either your straw-colour beard, your orange-tawny beard, your purple-in-grain beard, or your French-crown-colour beard, your perfect yellow.

QUINCE. Some of your French crowns have no hair at all, and then you will play bare-fac'd. But, masters, here are your parts; and I am to entreat you, request you, and desire you, to con them by to-morrow night; and meet me in the palace wood, a mile without the town, by moonlight; there will we rehearse; for if we meet in the city, we shall be dogg'd with company, and our devices known. In the meantime I will draw a bill of properties, such as our play wants. I pray you, fail me not.

Glance at my credit with Hippolyta,
Knowing I know thy love to Theseus?
Didst not thou lead him through the glimmering night
From Perigouna, whom he ravished?
And make him with fair Aegles break his faith,
With Ariadne and Antiopa?

TITANIA. These are the forgeries of jealousy;
    And never, since the middle summer's spring,
    Met we on hill, in dale, forest, or mead,
    By paved fountain, or by rushy brook,
    Or in the beached margent of the sea,
    To dance our ringlets to the whistling wind,
    But with thy brawls thou hast disturb'd our sport.
    Therefore the winds, piping to us in vain,
    As in revenge, have suck'd up from the sea
    Contagious fogs; which, falling in the land,
    Hath every pelting river made so proud
    That they have overborne their continents.
    The ox hath therefore stretch'd his yoke in vain,
    The ploughman lost his sweat, and the green corn
    Hath rotted ere his youth attain'd a beard;
    The fold stands empty in the drowned field,
    And crows are fatted with the murrion flock;
    The nine men's morris is fill'd up with mud,
    And the quaint mazes in the wanton green,
    For lack of tread, are undistinguishable.
    The human mortals want their winter here;
    No night is now with hymn or carol blest;
    Therefore the moon, the governess of floods,
    Pale in her anger, washes all the air,
    That rheumatic diseases do abound.
    And thorough this distemperature we see
    The seasons alter: hoary-headed frosts
    Fall in the fresh lap of the crimson rose;
    And on old Hiems' thin and icy crown

An odorous chaplet of sweet summer buds
Is, as in mockery, set. The spring, the summer,
The childing autumn, angry winter, change
Their wonted liveries; and the mazed world,
By their increase, now knows not which is which.
And this same progeny of evils comes
From our debate, from our dissension;
We are their parents and original.

OBERON. Do you amend it, then; it lies in you.
  Why should Titania cross her Oberon?
  I do but beg a little changeling boy
  To be my henchman.

TITANIA. Set your heart at rest;
  The fairy land buys not the child of me.
  His mother was a vot'ress of my order;
  And, in the spiced Indian air, by night,
  Full often hath she gossip'd by my side;
  And sat with me on Neptune's yellow sands,
  Marking th' embarked traders on the flood;
  When we have laugh'd to see the sails conceive,
  And grow big-bellied with the wanton wind;
  Which she, with pretty and with swimming gait
  Following- her womb then rich with my young squire-
  Would imitate, and sail upon the land,
  To fetch me trifles, and return again,
  As from a voyage, rich with merchandise.
  But she, being mortal, of that boy did die;
  And for her sake do I rear up her boy;
  And for her sake I will not part with him.

OBERON. How long within this wood intend you stay?

TITANIA. Perchance till after Theseus' wedding-day.
  If you will patiently dance in our round,

And see our moonlight revels, go with us;
If not, shun me, and I will spare your haunts.

OBERON. Give me that boy and I will go with thee.

TITANIA. Not for thy fairy kingdom. Fairies, away.
We shall chide downright if I longer stay.

[Exit TITANIA with her train]

OBERON. Well, go thy way; thou shalt not from this grove
Till I torment thee for this injury.
My gentle Puck, come hither. Thou rememb'rest
Since once I sat upon a promontory,
And heard a mermaid on a dolphin's back
Uttering such dulcet and harmonious breath
That the rude sea grew civil at her song,
And certain stars shot madly from their spheres
To hear the sea-maid's music.

PUCK. I remember.

OBERON. That very time I saw, but thou couldst not,
Flying between the cold moon and the earth
Cupid, all arm'd; a certain aim he took
At a fair vestal, throned by the west,
And loos'd his love-shaft smartly from his bow,
As it should pierce a hundred thousand hearts;
But I might see young Cupid's fiery shaft
Quench'd in the chaste beams of the wat'ry moon;
And the imperial vot'ress passed on,
In maiden meditation, fancy-free.
Yet mark'd I where the bolt of Cupid fell.
It fell upon a little western flower,
Before milk-white, now purple with love's wound,
And maidens call it Love-in-idleness.

Fetch me that flow'r, the herb I showed thee once.
The juice of it on sleeping eyelids laid
Will make or man or woman madly dote
Upon the next live creature that it sees.
Fetch me this herb, and be thou here again
Ere the leviathan can swim a league.

PUCK. I'll put a girdle round about the earth
In forty minutes.

[Exit PUCK]

OBERON. Having once this juice,
I'll watch Titania when she is asleep,
And drop the liquor of it in her eyes;
The next thing then she waking looks upon,
Be it on lion, bear, or wolf, or bull,
On meddling monkey, or on busy ape,
She shall pursue it with the soul of love.
And ere I take this charm from off her sight,
As I can take it with another herb,
I'll make her render up her page to me.
But who comes here? I am invisible;
And I will overhear their conference.

[Enter DEMETRIUS, HELENA following him]

DEMETRIUS. I love thee not, therefore pursue me not.
Where is Lysander and fair Hermia?
The one I'll slay, the other slayeth me.
Thou told'st me they were stol'n unto this wood,
And here am I, and wood within this wood,
Because I cannot meet my Hermia.
Hence, get thee gone, and follow me no more.

HELENA. You draw me, you hard-hearted adamant;

But yet you draw not iron, for my heart
Is true as steel. Leave you your power to draw,
And I shall have no power to follow you.

DEMETRIUS. Do I entice you? Do I speak you fair?
Or, rather, do I not in plainest truth
Tell you I do not nor I cannot love you?

HELENA. And even for that do I love you the more.
I am your spaniel; and, Demetrius,
The more you beat me, I will fawn on you.
Use me but as your spaniel, spurn me, strike me,
Neglect me, lose me; only give me leave,
Unworthy as I am, to follow you.
What worser place can I beg in your love,
And yet a place of high respect with me,
Than to be used as you use your dog?

DEMETRIUS. Tempt not too much the hatred of my spirit;
For I am sick when I do look on thee.

HELENA. And I am sick when I look not on you.

DEMETRIUS. You do impeach your modesty too much
To leave the city and commit yourself
Into the hands of one that loves you not;
To trust the opportunity of night,
And the ill counsel of a desert place,
With the rich worth of your virginity.

HELENA. Your virtue is my privilege for that:
It is not night when I do see your face,
Therefore I think I am not in the night;
Nor doth this wood lack worlds of company,
For you, in my respect, are all the world.
Then how can it be said I am alone

When all the world is here to look on me?

DEMETRIUS. I'll run from thee and hide me in the brakes,
And leave thee to the mercy of wild beasts.

HELENA. The wildest hath not such a heart as you.
Run when you will; the story shall be chang'd:
Apollo flies, and Daphne holds the chase;
The dove pursues the griffin; the mild hind
Makes speed to catch the tiger- bootless speed,
When cowardice pursues and valour flies.

DEMETRIUS. I will not stay thy questions; let me go;
Or, if thou follow me, do not believe
But I shall do thee mischief in the wood.

HELENA. Ay, in the temple, in the town, the field,
You do me mischief. Fie, Demetrius!
Your wrongs do set a scandal on my sex.
We cannot fight for love as men may do;
We should be woo'd, and were not made to woo.

[Exit DEMETRIUS]

HELENA. I'll follow thee, and make a heaven of hell,
To die upon the hand I love so well.

[Exit HELENA]

OBERON. Fare thee well, nymph; ere he do leave this grove,
Thou shalt fly him, and he shall seek thy love.

[Re-enter PUCK]

OBERON. Hast thou the flower there? Welcome, wanderer.

PUCK. Ay, there it is.

OBERON. I pray thee give it me.
　I know a bank where the wild thyme blows,
　Where oxlips and the nodding violet grows,
　Quite over-canopied with luscious woodbine,
　With sweet musk-roses, and with eglantine;
　There sleeps Titania sometime of the night,
　Lull'd in these flowers with dances and delight;
　And there the snake throws her enamell'd skin,
　Weed wide enough to wrap a fairy in;
　And with the juice of this I'll streak her eyes,
　And make her full of hateful fantasies.
　Take thou some of it, and seek through this grove:
　A sweet Athenian lady is in love
　With a disdainful youth; anoint his eyes;
　But do it when the next thing he espies
　May be the lady. Thou shalt know the man
　By the Athenian garments he hath on.
　Effect it with some care, that he may prove
　More fond on her than she upon her love.
　And look thou meet me ere the first cock crow.

PUCK. Fear not, my lord; your servant shall do so.

[Exeunt]

SCENE II. Another part of the wood

[Enter TITANIA, with her train]

TITANIA. Come now, a roundel and a fairy song;
　Then, for the third part of a minute, hence:
　Some to kill cankers in the musk-rose buds;
　Some war with rere-mice for their leathern wings,
　To make my small elves coats; and some keep back

The clamorous owl that nightly hoots and wonders
At our quaint spirits. Sing me now asleep;
Then to your offices, and let me rest.

[The FAIRIES Sing]

FIRST FAIRY. You spotted snakes with double tongue,
   Thorny hedgehogs, be not seen;
   Newts and blind-worms, do no wrong,
   Come not near our fairy Queen.

CHORUS. Philomel with melody
   Sing in our sweet lullaby.
   Lulla, lulla, lullaby; lulla, lulla, lullaby.
   Never harm
   Nor spell nor charm
   Come our lovely lady nigh.
   So good night, with lullaby.

SECOND FAIRY. Weaving spiders, come not here;
   Hence, you long-legg'd spinners, hence.
   Beetles black, approach not near;
   Worm nor snail do no offence.

CHORUS. Philomel with melody, etc.

[TITANIA Sleeps]

FIRST FAIRY. Hence away; now all is well.
   One aloof stand sentinel.

[Exeunt FAIRIES]

[Enter OBERON and squeezes the flower on TITANIA'S eyelids]

OBERON. What thou seest when thou dost wake,

For, as a surfeit of the sweetest things
The deepest loathing to the stomach brings,
Or as the heresies that men do leave
Are hated most of those they did deceive,
So thou, my surfeit and my heresy,
Of all be hated, but the most of me!
And, all my powers, address your love and might
To honour Helen, and to be her knight!

[Exit]

HERMIA. [Starting] Help me, Lysander, help me; do thy best
To pluck this crawling serpent from my breast.
Ay me, for pity! What a dream was here!
Lysander, look how I do quake with fear.
Methought a serpent eat my heart away,
And you sat smiling at his cruel prey.
Lysander! What, remov'd? Lysander! lord!
What, out of hearing gone? No sound, no word?
Alack, where are you? Speak, an if you hear;
Speak, of all loves! I swoon almost with fear.
No? Then I well perceive you are not nigh.
Either death or you I'll find immediately.

[Exit]

ACT III

ACT III. SCENE I. The wood. TITANIA lying asleep

[Enter QUINCE, SNUG, BOTTOM, FLUTE, SNOUT, and
STARVELING]

BOTTOM. Are we all met?

QUINCE. Pat, pat; and here's a marvellous convenient place for our
rehearsal. This green plot shall be our stage, this hawthorn brake our
tiring-house; and we will do it in action, as we will do it before
the Duke.

BOTTOM. Peter Quince!

QUINCE. What sayest thou, bully Bottom?

BOTTOM. There are things in this comedy of Pyramus and Thisby
that will never please. First, Pyramus must draw a sword to kill himself;
which the ladies cannot abide. How answer you that?

SNOUT. By'r lakin, a parlous fear.

STARVELING. I believe we must leave the killing out, when all is done.

BOTTOM. Not a whit; I have a device to make all well. Write me a prologue; and let the prologue seem to say we will do no harm with our swords, and that Pyramus is not kill'd indeed; and for the more better assurance, tell them that I Pyramus am not Pyramus but Bottom the weaver. This will put them out of fear.

QUINCE. Well, we will have such a prologue; and it shall be written in eight and six.

BOTTOM. No, make it two more; let it be written in eight and eight.

SNOUT. Will not the ladies be afeard of the lion?

STARVELING. I fear it, I promise you.

BOTTOM. Masters, you ought to consider with yourself to bring in- God shield us!- a lion among ladies is a most dreadful thing; for there is not a more fearful wild-fowl than your lion living; and we ought to look to't.

SNOUT. Therefore another prologue must tell he is not a lion.

BOTTOM. Nay, you must name his name, and half his face must be seen through the lion's neck; and he himself must speak through, saying thus, or to the same defect: 'Ladies,' or 'Fair ladies, I would wish you' or 'I would request you' or 'I would entreat you not to fear, not to tremble. My life for yours! If you think I come hither as a lion, it were pity of my life. No, I am no such thing; I am a man as other men are.' And there, indeed, let him name his name, and tell them plainly he is Snug the joiner.

QUINCE. Well, it shall be so. But there is two hard things- that is, to bring the moonlight into a chamber; for, you know, Pyramus and Thisby meet by moonlight.

SNOUT. Doth the moon shine that night we play our play?

BOTTOM. A calendar, a calendar! Look in the almanack; find out moonshine, find out moonshine.

QUINCE. Yes, it doth shine that night.

BOTTOM. Why, then may you leave a casement of the great chamber window, where we play, open; and the moon may shine in at the casement.

QUINCE. Ay; or else one must come in with a bush of thorns and a lantern, and say he comes to disfigure or to present the person of Moonshine. Then there is another thing: we must have a wall in the great chamber; for Pyramus and Thisby, says the story, did talk through the chink of a wall.

SNOUT. You can never bring in a wall. What say you, Bottom?

BOTTOM. Some man or other must present Wall; and let him have some plaster, or some loam, or some rough-cast about him, to signify wall; and let him hold his fingers thus, and through that cranny shall Pyramus and Thisby whisper.

QUINCE. If that may be, then all is well. Come, sit down, every mother's son, and rehearse your parts. Pyramus, you begin; when you have spoken your speech, enter into that brake; and so every one according to his cue.

[Enter PUCK behind]

PUCK. What hempen homespuns have we swagg'ring here,

So near the cradle of the Fairy Queen?
What, a play toward! I'll be an auditor;
An actor too perhaps, if I see cause.

QUINCE. Speak, Pyramus. Thisby, stand forth.

BOTTOM. Thisby, the flowers of odious savours sweet–

QUINCE. 'Odious'– odorous!

BOTTOM. –odours savours sweet;
   So hath thy breath, my dearest Thisby dear.
   But hark, a voice! Stay thou but here awhile,
   And by and by I will to thee appear.

[Exit]

PUCK. A stranger Pyramus than e'er played here!

[Exit]

FLUTE. Must I speak now?

QUINCE. Ay, marry, must you; for you must understand he goes but
to see a noise that he heard, and is to come again.

FLUTE. Most radiant Pyramus, most lily-white of hue,
   Of colour like the red rose on triumphant brier,
   Most brisky juvenal, and eke most lovely Jew,
   As true as truest horse, that would never tire,
   I'll meet thee, Pyramus, at Ninny's tomb.

QUINCE. 'Ninus' tomb,' man! Why, you must not speak that yet; that
you answer to Pyramus. You speak all your part at once, cues, and all.
Pyramus enter: your cue is past; it is 'never tire.'

FLUTE. O- As true as truest horse, that y et would never tire.

[Re-enter PUCK, and BOTTOM with an ass's head]

BOTTOM. If I were fair, Thisby, I were only thine.

QUINCE. O monstrous! O strange! We are haunted. Pray, masters! Fly, masters! Help!

[Exeunt all but BOTTOM and PUCK]

PUCK. I'll follow you; I'll lead you about a round,
    Through bog, through bush, through brake, through brier;
    Sometime a horse I'll be, sometime a hound,
    A hog, a headless bear, sometime a fire;
    And neigh, and bark, and grunt, and roar, and burn,
    Like horse, hound, hog, bear, fire, at every turn.

[Exit]

BOTTOM. Why do they run away? This is a knavery of them to make me afeard.

[Re-enter SNOUT]

SNOUT. O Bottom, thou art chang'd! What do I see on thee?

BOTTOM. What do you see? You see an ass-head of your own, do you?

[Exit SNOUT]

[Re-enter QUINCE]

QUINCE. Bless thee, Bottom, bless thee! Thou art translated.

[Exit]

BOTTOM. I see their knavery: this is to make an ass of me; to fright me, if they could. But I will not stir from this place, do what they can; I will walk up and down here, and will sing, that they shall hear I am not afraid.
[Sings] The ousel cock, so black of hue,
  With orange-tawny bill,
  The throstle with his note so true,
  The wren with little quill.

TITANIA. What angel wakes me from my flow'ry bed?

BOTTOM. [Sings] The finch, the sparrow, and the lark,
  The plain-song cuckoo grey,
  Whose note full many a man doth mark,
  And dares not answer nay-
for, indeed, who would set his wit to so foolish a bird? Who would give a bird the he, though he cry 'cuckoo' never so?

TITANIA. I pray thee, gentle mortal, sing again.
 Mine ear is much enamoured of thy note;
 So is mine eye enthralled to thy shape;
 And thy fair virtue's force perforce doth move me,
 On the first view, to say, to swear, I love thee.

BOTTOM. Methinks, mistress, you should have little reason for that. And yet, to say the truth, reason and love keep little company together now-a-days. The more the pity that some honest neighbours will not make them friends. Nay, I can gleek upon occasion.

TITANIA. Thou art as wise as thou art beautiful.

BOTTOM. Not so, neither; but if I had wit enough to get out of this wood, I have enough to serve mine own turn.

TITANIA. Out of this wood do not desire to go;
   Thou shalt remain here whether thou wilt or no.
   I am a spirit of no common rate;
   The summer still doth tend upon my state;
   And I do love thee; therefore, go with me.
   I'll give thee fairies to attend on thee;
   And they shall fetch thee jewels from the deep,
   And sing, while thou on pressed flowers dost sleep;
   And I will purge thy mortal grossness so
   That thou shalt like an airy spirit go.
   Peaseblossom! Cobweb! Moth! and Mustardseed!

[Enter PEASEBLOSSOM, COBWEB, MOTH, and
MUSTARDSEED]

PEASEBLOSSOM. Ready.

COBWEB. And I.

MOTH. And I.

MUSTARDSEED. And I.

ALL. Where shall we go?

TITANIA. Be kind and courteous to this gentleman;
   Hop in his walks and gambol in his eyes;
   Feed him with apricocks and dewberries,
   With purple grapes, green figs, and mulberries;
   The honey bags steal from the humble-bees,
   And for night-tapers crop their waxen thighs,
   And light them at the fiery glow-worm's eyes,
   To have my love to bed and to arise;
   And pluck the wings from painted butterflies,
   To fan the moonbeams from his sleeping eyes.
   Nod to him, elves, and do him courtesies.

PEASEBLOSSOM. Hail, mortal!

COBWEB. Hail!

MOTH. Hail!

MUSTARDSEED. Hail!

BOTTOM. I cry your worships mercy, heartily; I beseech your worship's name.

COBWEB. Cobweb.

BOTTOM. I shall desire you of more acquaintance, good Master Cobweb. If I cut my finger, I shall make bold with you. Your name, honest gentleman?

PEASEBLOSSOM. Peaseblossom.

BOTTOM. I pray you, commend me to Mistress Squash, your mother, and to Master Peascod, your father. Good Master Peaseblossom, I shall desire you of more acquaintance too. Your name, I beseech you, sir?

MUSTARDSEED. Mustardseed.

BOTTOM. Good Master Mustardseed, I know your patience well. That same cowardly giant-like ox-beef hath devour'd many a gentleman of your house. I promise you your kindred hath made my eyes water ere now. I desire you of more acquaintance, good Master Mustardseed.

TITANIA. Come, wait upon him; lead him to my bower.
    The moon, methinks, looks with a wat'ry eye;
    And when she weeps, weeps every little flower;
    Lamenting some enforced chastity.
    Tie up my love's tongue, bring him silently.

[Exeunt]

SCENE II. Another part of the wood

[Enter OBERON]

OBERON. I wonder if Titania be awak'd;
  Then, what it was that next came in her eye,
  Which she must dote on in extremity.

[Enter PUCK]

OBERON. Here comes my messenger. How now, mad spirit!
  What night-rule now about this haunted grove?

PUCK. My mistress with a monster is in love.
  Near to her close and consecrated bower,
  While she was in her dull and sleeping hour,
  A crew of patches, rude mechanicals,
  That work for bread upon Athenian stalls,
  Were met together to rehearse a play
  Intended for great Theseus' nuptial day.
  The shallowest thickskin of that barren sort,
  Who Pyramus presented, in their sport
  Forsook his scene and ent'red in a brake;
  When I did him at this advantage take,
  An ass's nole I fixed on his head.
  Anon his Thisby must be answered,
  And forth my mimic comes. When they him spy,
  As wild geese that the creeping fowler eye,
  Or russet-pated choughs, many in sort,
  Rising and cawing at the gun's report,
  Sever themselves and madly sweep the sky,
  So at his sight away his fellows fly;
  And at our stamp here, o'er and o'er one falls;
  He murder cries, and help from Athens calls.

Their sense thus weak, lost with their fears thus strong,
Made senseless things begin to do them wrong,
For briers and thorns at their apparel snatch;
Some sleeves, some hats, from yielders all things catch.
I led them on in this distracted fear,
And left sweet Pyramus translated there;
When in that moment, so it came to pass,
Titania wak'd, and straightway lov'd an ass.

OBERON. This falls out better than I could devise.
  But hast thou yet latch'd the Athenian's eyes
  With the love-juice, as I did bid thee do?

PUCK. I took him sleeping- that is finish'd too-
  And the Athenian woman by his side;
  That, when he wak'd, of force she must be ey'd.

[Enter DEMETRIUS and HERMIA]

OBERON. Stand close; this is the same Athenian.

PUCK. This is the woman, but not this the man.

DEMETRIUS. O, why rebuke you him that loves you so?
  Lay breath so bitter on your bitter foe.

HERMIA. Now I but chide, but I should use thee worse,
  For thou, I fear, hast given me cause to curse.
  If thou hast slain Lysander in his sleep,
  Being o'er shoes in blood, plunge in the deep,
  And kill me too.
  The sun was not so true unto the day
  As he to me. Would he have stolen away
  From sleeping Hermia? I'll believe as soon
  This whole earth may be bor'd, and that the moon
  May through the centre creep and so displease

Her brother's noontide with th' Antipodes.
It cannot be but thou hast murd'red him;
So should a murderer look- so dead, so grim.

DEMETRIUS. So should the murdered look; and so should I,
   Pierc'd through the heart with your stern cruelty;
   Yet you, the murderer, look as bright, as clear,
   As yonder Venus in her glimmering sphere.

HERMIA. What's this to my Lysander? Where is he?
   Ah, good Demetrius, wilt thou give him me?

DEMETRIUS. I had rather give his carcass to my hounds.

HERMIA. Out, dog! out, cur! Thou driv'st me past the bounds
   Of maiden's patience. Hast thou slain him, then?
   Henceforth be never numb'red among men!
   O, once tell true; tell true, even for my sake!
   Durst thou have look'd upon him being awake,
   And hast thou kill'd him sleeping? O brave touch!
   Could not a worm, an adder, do so much?
   An adder did it; for with doubler tongue
   Than thine, thou serpent, never adder stung.

DEMETRIUS. You spend your passion on a mispris'd mood:
   I am not guilty of Lysander's blood;
   Nor is he dead, for aught that I can tell.

HERMIA. I pray thee, tell me then that he is well.

DEMETRIUS. An if I could, what should I get therefore?

HERMIA. A privilege never to see me more.
   And from thy hated presence part I so;
   See me no more whether he be dead or no.

DEMETRIUS. There is no following her in this fierce vein;
  Here, therefore, for a while I will remain.
  So sorrow's heaviness doth heavier grow
  For debt that bankrupt sleep doth sorrow owe;
  Which now in some slight measure it will pay,
  If for his tender here I make some stay.

[Lies down]

OBERON. What hast thou done? Thou hast mistaken quite,
  And laid the love-juice on some true-love's sight.
  Of thy misprision must perforce ensue
  Some true love turn'd, and not a false turn'd true.

PUCK. Then fate o'er-rules, that, one man holding troth,
  A million fail, confounding oath on oath.

OBERON. About the wood go swifter than the wind,
  And Helena of Athens look thou find;
  All fancy-sick she is and pale of cheer,
  With sighs of love that costs the fresh blood dear.
  By some illusion see thou bring her here;
  I'll charm his eyes against she do appear.

PUCK. I go, I go; look how I go,
  Swifter than arrow from the Tartar's bow.

[Exit]

OBERON. Flower of this purple dye,
      Hit with Cupid's archery,
      Sink in apple of his eye.
      When his love he doth espy,
      Let her shine as gloriously

As the Venus of the sky.
When thou wak'st, if she be by,
Beg of her for remedy.

[Re-enter PUCK]

PUCK. Captain of our fairy band,
Helena is here at hand,
And the youth mistook by me
Pleading for a lover's fee;
Shall we their fond pageant see?
Lord, what fools these mortals be!

OBERON. Stand aside. The noise they make
Will cause Demetrius to awake.

PUCK. Then will two at once woo one.
That must needs be sport alone;
And those things do best please me
That befall prepost'rously.

[Enter LYSANDER and HELENA]

LYSANDER. Why should you think that I should woo in scorn?
Scorn and derision never come in tears.
Look when I vow, I weep; and vows so born,
In their nativity all truth appears.
How can these things in me seem scorn to you,
Bearing the badge of faith, to prove them true?

HELENA. You do advance your cunning more and more.
When truth kills truth, O devilish-holy fray!
These vows are Hermia's. Will you give her o'er?
Weigh oath with oath, and you will nothing weigh:
Your vows to her and me, put in two scales,
Will even weigh; and both as light as tales.

LYSANDER. I hod no judgment when to her I swore.

HELENA. Nor none, in my mind, now you give her o'er.

LYSANDER. Demetrius loves her, and he loves not you.

DEMETRIUS. [Awaking] O Helen, goddess, nymph, perfect, divine!
    To what, my love, shall I compare thine eyne?
    Crystal is muddy. O, how ripe in show
    Thy lips, those kissing cherries, tempting grow!
    That pure congealed white, high Taurus' snow,
    Fann'd with the eastern wind, turns to a crow
    When thou hold'st up thy hand. O, let me kiss
    This princess of pure white, this seal of bliss!

HELENA. O spite! O hell! I see you all are bent
    To set against me for your merriment.
    If you were civil and knew courtesy,
    You would not do me thus much injury.
    Can you not hate me, as I know you do,
    But you must join in souls to mock me too?
    If you were men, as men you are in show,
    You would not use a gentle lady so:
    To vow, and swear, and superpraise my parts,
    When I am sure you hate me with your hearts.
    You both are rivals, and love Hermia;
    And now both rivals, to mock Helena.
    A trim exploit, a manly enterprise,
    To conjure tears up in a poor maid's eyes
    With your derision! None of noble sort
    Would so offend a virgin, and extort
    A poor soul's patience, all to make you sport.

LYSANDER. You are unkind, Demetrius; be not so;
    For you love Hermia. This you know I know;
    And here, with all good will, with all my heart,

In Hermia's love I yield you up my part;
And yours of Helena to me bequeath,
Whom I do love and will do till my death.

HELENA. Never did mockers waste more idle breath.

DEMETRIUS. Lysander, keep thy Hermia; I will none.
    If e'er I lov'd her, all that love is gone.
    My heart to her but as guest-wise sojourn'd,
    And now to Helen is it home return'd,
    There to remain.

LYSANDER. Helen, it is not so.

DEMETRIUS. Disparage not the faith thou dost not know,
    Lest, to thy peril, thou aby it dear.
    Look where thy love comes; yonder is thy dear.

[Enter HERMIA]

HERMIA. Dark night, that from the eye his function takes,
    The ear more quick of apprehension makes;
    Wherein it doth impair the seeing sense,
    It pays the hearing double recompense.
    Thou art not by mine eye, Lysander, found;
    Mine ear, I thank it, brought me to thy sound.
    But why unkindly didst thou leave me so?

LYSANDER. Why should he stay whom love doth press to go?

HERMIA. What love could press Lysander from my side?

LYSANDER. Lysander's love, that would not let him bide-
    Fair Helena, who more engilds the night
    Than all yon fiery oes and eyes of light.
    Why seek'st thou me? Could not this make thee know

The hate I bare thee made me leave thee so?

HERMIA. You speak not as you think; it cannot be.

HELENA. Lo, she is one of this confederacy!
    Now I perceive they have conjoin'd all three
    To fashion this false sport in spite of me.
    Injurious Hermia! most ungrateful maid!
    Have you conspir'd, have you with these contriv'd,
    To bait me with this foul derision?
    Is all the counsel that we two have shar'd,
    The sisters' vows, the hours that we have spent,
    When we have chid the hasty-footed time
    For parting us- O, is all forgot?
    All school-days' friendship, childhood innocence?
    We, Hermia, like two artificial gods,
    Have with our needles created both one flower,
    Both on one sampler, sitting on one cushion,
    Both warbling of one song, both in one key;
    As if our hands, our sides, voices, and minds,
    Had been incorporate. So we grew together,
    Like to a double cherry, seeming parted,
    But yet an union in partition,
    Two lovely berries moulded on one stern;
    So, with two seeming bodies, but one heart;
    Two of the first, like coats in heraldry,
    Due but to one, and crowned with one crest.
    And will you rent our ancient love asunder,
    To join with men in scorning your poor friend?
    It is not friendly, 'tis not maidenly;
    Our sex, as well as I, may chide you for it,
    Though I alone do feel the injury.

HERMIA. I am amazed at your passionate words;
    I scorn you not; it seems that you scorn me.

HELENA. Have you not set Lysander, as in scorn,
    To follow me and praise my eyes and face?
    And made your other love, Demetrius,
    Who even but now did spurn me with his foot,
    To call me goddess, nymph, divine, and rare,
    Precious, celestial? Wherefore speaks he this
    To her he hates? And wherefore doth Lysander
    Deny your love, so rich within his soul,
    And tender me, forsooth, affection,
    But by your setting on, by your consent?
    What though I be not so in grace as you,
    So hung upon with love, so fortunate,
    But miserable most, to love unlov'd?
    This you should pity rather than despise.

HERMIA. I understand not what you mean by this.

HELENA. Ay, do- persever, counterfeit sad looks,
    Make mouths upon me when I turn my back,
    Wink each at other; hold the sweet jest up;
    This sport, well carried, shall be chronicled.
    If you have any pity, grace, or manners,
    You would not make me such an argument.
    But fare ye well; 'tis partly my own fault,
    Which death, or absence, soon shall remedy.

LYSANDER. Stay, gentle Helena; hear my excuse;
    My love, my life, my soul, fair Helena!

HELENA. O excellent!

HERMIA. Sweet, do not scorn her so.

DEMETRIUS. If she cannot entreat, I can compel.

LYSANDER. Thou canst compel no more than she entreat;

Thy threats have no more strength than her weak prayers
Helen, I love thee, by my life I do;
I swear by that which I will lose for thee
To prove him false that says I love thee not.

DEMETRIUS. I say I love thee more than he can do.

LYSANDER. If thou say so, withdraw, and prove it too.

DEMETRIUS. Quick, come.

HERMIA. Lysander, whereto tends all this?

LYSANDER. Away, you Ethiope!

DEMETRIUS. No, no, he will
   Seem to break loose- take on as you would follow,
   But yet come not. You are a tame man; go!

LYSANDER. Hang off, thou cat, thou burr; vile thing, let loose,
   Or I will shake thee from me like a serpent.

HERMIA. Why are you grown so rude? What change is this,
   Sweet love?

LYSANDER. Thy love! Out, tawny Tartar, out!
   Out, loathed med'cine! O hated potion, hence!

HERMIA. Do you not jest?

HELENA. Yes, sooth; and so do you.

LYSANDER. Demetrius, I will keep my word with thee.

DEMETRIUS. I would I had your bond; for I perceive
   A weak bond holds you; I'll not trust your word.

LYSANDER. What, should I hurt her, strike her, kill her dead?
Although I hate her, I'll not harm her so.

HERMIA. What! Can you do me greater harm than hate?
Hate me! wherefore? O me! what news, my love?
Am not I Hermia? Are not you Lysander?
I am as fair now as I was erewhile.
Since night you lov'd me; yet since night you left me.
Why then, you left me- O, the gods forbid!-
In earnest, shall I say?

LYSANDER. Ay, by my life!
And never did desire to see thee more.
Therefore be out of hope, of question, of doubt;
Be certain, nothing truer; 'tis no jest
That I do hate thee and love Helena.

HERMIA. O me! you juggler! you cankerblossom!
You thief of love! What! Have you come by night,
And stol'n my love's heart from him?

HELENA. Fine, i' faith!
Have you no modesty, no maiden shame,
No touch of bashfulness? What! Will you tear
Impatient answers from my gentle tongue?
Fie, fie! you counterfeit, you puppet you!

HERMIA. 'Puppet!' why so? Ay, that way goes the game.
Now I perceive that she hath made compare
Between our statures; she hath urg'd her height;
And with her personage, her tall personage,
Her height, forsooth, she hath prevail'd with him.
And are you grown so high in his esteem
Because I am so dwarfish and so low?
How low am I, thou painted maypole? Speak.
How low am I? I am not yet so low

But that my nails can reach unto thine eyes.

HELENA. I pray you, though you mock me, gentlemen,
Let her not hurt me. I was never curst;
I have no gift at all in shrewishness;
I am a right maid for my cowardice;
Let her not strike me. You perhaps may think,
Because she is something lower than myself,
That I can match her.

HERMIA. 'Lower' hark, again.

HELENA. Good Hermia, do not be so bitter with me.
I evermore did love you, Hermia,
Did ever keep your counsels, never wrong'd you;
Save that, in love unto Demetrius,
I told him of your stealth unto this wood.
He followed you; for love I followed him;
But he hath chid me hence, and threat'ned me
To strike me, spurn me, nay, to kill me too;
And now, so you will let me quiet go,
To Athens will I bear my folly back,
And follow you no further. Let me go.
You see how simple and how fond I am.

HERMIA. Why, get you gone! Who is't that hinders you?

HELENA. A foolish heart that I leave here behind.

HERMIA. What! with Lysander?

HELENA. With Demetrius.

LYSANDER. Be not afraid; she shall not harm thee, Helena.

DEMETRIUS. No, sir, she shall not, though you take her part.

HELENA. O, when she is angry, she is keen and shrewd;
　　She was a vixen when she went to school;
　　And, though she be but little, she is fierce.

HERMIA. 'Little' again! Nothing but 'low' and 'little'!
　　Why will you suffer her to flout me thus?
　　Let me come to her.

LYSANDER. Get you gone, you dwarf;
　　You minimus, of hind'ring knot-grass made;
　　You bead, you acorn.

DEMETRIUS. You are too officious
　　In her behalf that scorns your services.
　　Let her alone; speak not of Helena;
　　Take not her part; for if thou dost intend
　　Never so little show of love to her,
　　Thou shalt aby it.

LYSANDER. Now she holds me not.
　　Now follow, if thou dar'st, to try whose right,
　　Of thine or mine, is most in Helena.

DEMETRIUS. Follow! Nay, I'll go with thee, cheek by jowl.

[Exeunt LYSANDER and DEMETRIUS]

HERMIA. You, mistress, all this coil is long of you.
　　Nay, go not back.

HELENA. I will not trust you, I;
　　Nor longer stay in your curst company.
　　Your hands than mine are quicker for a fray;
　　My legs are longer though, to run away.

[Exit]

HERMIA. I am amaz'd, and know not what to say.

[Exit]

OBERON. This is thy negligence. Still thou mistak'st,
  Or else committ'st thy knaveries wilfully.

PUCK. Believe me, king of shadows, I mistook.
  Did not you tell me I should know the man
  By the Athenian garments he had on?
  And so far blameless proves my enterprise
  That I have 'nointed an Athenian's eyes;
  And so far am I glad it so did sort,
  As this their jangling I esteem a sport.

OBERON. Thou seest these lovers seek a place to fight.
  Hie therefore, Robin, overcast the night;
  The starry welkin cover thou anon
  With drooping fog as black as Acheron,
  And lead these testy rivals so astray
  As one come not within another's way.
  Like to Lysander sometime frame thy tongue,
  Then stir Demetrius up with bitter wrong;
  And sometime rail thou like Demetrius;
  And from each other look thou lead them thus,
  Till o'er their brows death-counterfeiting sleep
  With leaden legs and batty wings doth creep.
  Then crush this herb into Lysander's eye;
  Whose liquor hath this virtuous property,
  To take from thence all error with his might
  And make his eyeballs roll with wonted sight.
  When they next wake, all this derision
  Shall seem a dream and fruitless vision;
  And back to Athens shall the lovers wend
  With league whose date till death shall never end.
  Whiles I in this affair do thee employ,

I'll to my queen, and beg her Indian boy;
And then I will her charmed eye release
From monster's view, and all things shall be peace.

PUCK. My fairy lord, this must be done with haste,
For night's swift dragons cut the clouds full fast;
And yonder shines Aurora's harbinger,
At whose approach ghosts, wand'ring here and there,
Troop home to churchyards. Damned spirits all
That in cross-ways and floods have burial,
Already to their wormy beds are gone,
For fear lest day should look their shames upon;
They wilfully themselves exil'd from light,
And must for aye consort with black-brow'd night.

OBERON. But we are spirits of another sort:
I with the Morning's love have oft made sport;
And, like a forester, the groves may tread
Even till the eastern gate, all fiery red,
Opening on Neptune with fair blessed beams,
Turns into yellow gold his salt green streams.
But, notwithstanding, haste, make no delay;
We may effect this business yet ere day.

[Exit OBERON]

PUCK. Up and down, up and down,
   I will lead them up and down.
   I am fear'd in field and town.
   Goblin, lead them up and down.
  Here comes one.

[Enter LYSANDER]

LYSANDER. Where art thou, proud Demetrius? Speak thou now.

PUCK. Here, villain, drawn and ready. Where art thou?

LYSANDER. I will be with thee straight.

PUCK. Follow me, then,
　　To plainer ground.

　　　　　　　　　　　[Exit LYSANDER as following the voice]

　　　　　　　　　[Enter DEMETRIUS]

DEMETRIUS. Lysander, speak again.
　　Thou runaway, thou coward, art thou fled?
　　Speak! In some bush? Where dost thou hide thy head?

PUCK. Thou coward, art thou bragging to the stars,
　　Telling the bushes that thou look'st for wars,
　　And wilt not come? Come, recreant, come, thou child;
　　I'll whip thee with a rod. He is defil'd
　　That draws a sword on thee.

DEMETRIUS. Yea, art thou there?

PUCK. Follow my voice; we'll try no manhood here.

　　　　　　　　　　　　　　　　　　[Exeunt]

　　　　　　　　　[Re-enter LYSANDER]

LYSANDER. He goes before me, and still dares me on;
　　When I come where he calls, then he is gone.
　　The villain is much lighter heel'd than I.
　　I followed fast, but faster he did fly,
　　That fallen am I in dark uneven way,
　　And here will rest me. [Lies down] Come, thou gentle day.
　　For if but once thou show me thy grey light,

I'll find Demetrius, and revenge this spite.

[Sleeps]

[Re-enter PUCK and DEMETRIUS]

PUCK. Ho, ho, ho! Coward, why com'st thou not?

DEMETRIUS. Abide me, if thou dar'st; for well I wot
   Thou run'st before me, shifting every place,
   And dar'st not stand, nor look me in the face.
   Where art thou now?

PUCK. Come hither; I am here.

DEMETRIUS. Nay, then, thou mock'st me. Thou shalt buy this dear,
   If ever I thy face by daylight see;
   Now, go thy way. Faintness constraineth me
   To measure out my length on this cold bed.
   By day's approach look to be visited.

[Lies down and sleeps]

[Enter HELENA]

HELENA. O weary night, O long and tedious night,
   Abate thy hours! Shine comforts from the east,
   That I may back to Athens by daylight,
   From these that my poor company detest.
   And sleep, that sometimes shuts up sorrow's eye,
   Steal me awhile from mine own company.

[Sleeps]

PUCK. Yet but three? Come one more;
   Two of both kinds makes up four.

Here she comes, curst and sad.
Cupid is a knavish lad,
Thus to make poor females mad.

[Enter HERMIA]

HERMIA. Never so weary, never so in woe,
Bedabbled with the dew, and torn with briers,
I can no further crawl, no further go;
My legs can keep no pace with my desires.
Here will I rest me till the break of day.
Heavens shield Lysander, if they mean a fray!

[Lies down and sleeps]

PUCK. On the ground
Sleep sound;
I'll apply
To your eye,
Gentle lover, remedy.

[Squeezing the juice on LYSANDER'S eyes]

PUCK. When thou wak'st,
Thou tak'st
True delight
In the sight
Of thy former lady's eye;
And the country proverb known,
That every man should take his own,
In your waking shall be shown:
Jack shall have Jill;
Nought shall go ill;
The man shall have his mare again, and all shall be well.

[Exit]

ACT IV

ACT IV. SCENE I. The wood. LYSANDER, DEMETRIUS, HELENA, and HERMIA, lying asleep

[Enter TITANIA and Bottom; PEASEBLOSSOM, COBWEB, MOTH, MUSTARDSEED, and other FAIRIES attending; OBERON behind, unseen]

TITANIA. Come, sit thee down upon this flow'ry bed,
  While I thy amiable cheeks do coy,
  And stick musk-roses in thy sleek smooth head,
  And kiss thy fair large ears, my gentle joy.

BOTTOM. Where's Peaseblossom?

PEASEBLOSSOM. Ready.

BOTTOM. Scratch my head, Peaseblossom.
  Where's Mounsieur Cobweb?

COBWEB. Ready.

BOTTOM. Mounsieur Cobweb; good mounsieur, get you your weapons in your hand and kill me a red-hipp'd humble-bee on the top of a thistle; and, good mounsieur, bring me the honey-bag. Do not fret yourself too much in the action, mounsieur; and, good mounsieur, have a care the honey-bag break not; I would be loath to have you over-flown with a honey-bag, signior. Where's Mounsieur Mustardseed?

MUSTARDSEED. Ready.

BOTTOM. Give me your neaf, Mounsieur Mustardseed. Pray you, leave your curtsy, good mounsieur.

MUSTARDSEED. What's your will?

BOTTOM. Nothing, good mounsieur, but to help Cavalery Cobweb to scratch. I must to the barber's, mounsieur; for methinks I am marvellous hairy about the face; and I am such a tender ass, if my hair do but tickle me I must scratch.

TITANIA. What, wilt thou hear some music, my sweet love?

BOTTOM. I have a reasonable good ear in music. Let's have the tongs and the bones.

TITANIA. Or say, sweet love, what thou desirest to eat.

BOTTOM. Truly, a peck of provender; I could munch your good dry oats. Methinks I have a great desire to a bottle of hay. Good hay, sweet hay, hath no fellow.

TITANIA. I have a venturous fairy that shall seek
    The squirrel's hoard, and fetch thee new nuts.

BOTTOM. I had rather have a handful or two of dried peas. But, pray you, let none of your people stir me; I have an exposition of sleep come upon me.

TITANIA. Sleep thou, and I will wind thee in my arms.
   Fairies, be gone, and be all ways away. Exeunt FAIRIES
   So doth the woodbine the sweet honeysuckle
   Gently entwist; the female ivy so
   Enrings the barky fingers of the elm.
   O, how I love thee! how I dote on thee!

[They sleep]

[Enter PUCK]

OBERON. [Advancing] Welcome, good Robin. Seest thou
   this sweet sight?
   Her dotage now I do begin to pity;
   For, meeting her of late behind the wood,
   Seeking sweet favours for this hateful fool,
   I did upbraid her and fall out with her.
   For she his hairy temples then had rounded
   With coronet of fresh and fragrant flowers;
   And that same dew which sometime on the buds
   Was wont to swell like round and orient pearls
   Stood now within the pretty flowerets' eyes,
   Like tears that did their own disgrace bewail.
   When I had at my pleasure taunted her,
   And she in mild terms begg'd my patience,
   I then did ask of her her changeling child;
   Which straight she gave me, and her fairy sent
   To bear him to my bower in fairy land.
   And now I have the boy, I will undo
   This hateful imperfection of her eyes.
   And, gentle Puck, take this transformed scalp
   From off the head of this Athenian swain,
   That he awaking when the other do
   May all to Athens back again repair,
   And think no more of this night's accidents
   But as the fierce vexation of a dream.

But first I will release the Fairy Queen.

[Touching her eyes]

OBERON. Be as thou wast wont to be;
   See as thou was wont to see.
   Dian's bud o'er Cupid's flower
   Hath such force and blessed power.
   Now, my Titania; wake you, my sweet queen.

TITANIA. My Oberon! What visions have I seen!
   Methought I was enamour'd of an ass.

OBERON. There lies your love.

TITANIA. How came these things to pass?
   O, how mine eyes do loathe his visage now!

OBERON. Silence awhile. Robin, take off this head.
   Titania, music call; and strike more dead
   Than common sleep of all these five the sense.

TITANIA. Music, ho, music, such as charmeth sleep!

PUCK. Now when thou wak'st with thine own fool's eyes peep.

OBERON. Sound, music. Come, my Queen, take hands with me,

[Music]

OBERON. And rock the ground whereon these sleepers be.
   Now thou and I are new in amity,
   And will to-morrow midnight solemnly
   Dance in Duke Theseus' house triumphantly,
   And bless it to all fair prosperity.
   There shall the pairs of faithful lovers be

Wedded, with Theseus, an in jollity.

PUCK. Fairy King, attend and mark;
      I do hear the morning lark.

OBERON. Then, my Queen, in silence sad,
      Trip we after night's shade.
      We the globe can compass soon,
      Swifter than the wand'ring moon.

TITANIA. Come, my lord; and in our flight,
      Tell me how it came this night
      That I sleeping here was found
      With these mortals on the ground.

[Exeunt]

[To the winding of horns, enter THESEUS, HIPPOLYTA,
EGEUS, and train]

THESEUS. Go, one of you, find out the forester;
      For now our observation is perform'd,
      And since we have the vaward of the day,
      My love shall hear the music of my hounds.
      Uncouple in the western valley; let them go.
      Dispatch, I say, and find the forester.

[Exit an ATTENDANT]

THESEUS. We will, fair Queen, up to the mountain's top,
      And mark the musical confusion
      Of hounds and echo in conjunction.

HIPPOLYTA. I was with Hercules and Cadmus once
      When in a wood of Crete they bay'd the bear
      With hounds of Sparta; never did I hear

Such gallant chiding, for, besides the groves,
The skies, the fountains, every region near
Seem'd all one mutual cry. I never heard
So musical a discord, such sweet thunder.

THESEUS. My hounds are bred out of the Spartan kind,
   So flew'd, so sanded; and their heads are hung
   With ears that sweep away the morning dew;
   Crook-knee'd and dew-lapp'd like Thessalian bulls;
   Slow in pursuit, but match'd in mouth like bells,
   Each under each. A cry more tuneable
   Was never holla'd to, nor cheer'd with horn,
   In Crete, in Sparta, nor in Thessaly.
   Judge when you hear. But, soft, what nymphs are these?

EGEUS. My lord, this is my daughter here asleep,
   And this Lysander, this Demetrius is,
   This Helena, old Nedar's Helena.
   I wonder of their being here together.

THESEUS. No doubt they rose up early to observe
   The rite of May; and, hearing our intent,
   Came here in grace of our solemnity.
   But speak, Egeus; is not this the day
   That Hermia should give answer of her choice?

EGEUS. It is, my lord.

THESEUS. Go, bid the huntsmen wake them with their horns.

             [Horns and shout within. The sleepers
                        awake and kneel to THESEUS]

THESEUS. Good-morrow, friends. Saint Valentine is past;
   Begin these wood-birds but to couple now?

LYSANDER. Pardon, my lord.

THESEUS. I pray you all, stand up.
  I know you two are rival enemies;
  How comes this gentle concord in the world
  That hatred is so far from jealousy
  To sleep by hate, and fear no enmity?

LYSANDER. My lord, I shall reply amazedly,
  Half sleep, half waking; but as yet, I swear,
  I cannot truly say how I came here,
  But, as I think- for truly would I speak,
  And now I do bethink me, so it is-
  I came with Hermia hither. Our intent
  Was to be gone from Athens, where we might,
  Without the peril of the Athenian law-

EGEUS. Enough, enough, my Lord; you have enough;
  I beg the law, the law upon his head.
  They would have stol'n away, they would, Demetrius,
  Thereby to have defeated you and me:
  You of your wife, and me of my consent,
  Of my consent that she should be your wife.

DEMETRIUS. My lord, fair Helen told me of their stealth,
  Of this their purpose hither to this wood;
  And I in fury hither followed them,
  Fair Helena in fancy following me.
  But, my good lord, I wot not by what power-
  But by some power it is- my love to Hermia,
  Melted as the snow, seems to me now
  As the remembrance of an idle gaud
  Which in my childhood I did dote upon;
  And all the faith, the virtue of my heart,
  The object and the pleasure of mine eye,
  Is only Helena. To her, my lord,

Was I betroth'd ere I saw Hermia.
But, like a sickness, did I loathe this food;
But, as in health, come to my natural taste,
Now I do wish it, love it, long for it,
And will for evermore be true to it.

THESEUS. Fair lovers, you are fortunately met;
Of this discourse we more will hear anon.
Egeus, I will overbear your will;
For in the temple, by and by, with us
These couples shall eternally be knit.
And, for the morning now is something worn,
Our purpos'd hunting shall be set aside.
Away with us to Athens, three and three;
We'll hold a feast in great solemnity.
Come, Hippolyta.

[Exeunt THESEUS, HIPPOLYTA, EGEUS, and train]

DEMETRIUS. These things seem small and undistinguishable,
Like far-off mountains turned into clouds.

HERMIA. Methinks I see these things with parted eye,
When every thing seems double.

HELENA. So methinks;
And I have found Demetrius like a jewel,
Mine own, and not mine own.

DEMETRIUS. Are you sure
That we are awake? It seems to me
That yet we sleep, we dream. Do not you think
The Duke was here, and bid us follow him?

HERMIA. Yea, and my father.

HELENA. And Hippolyta.

LYSANDER. And he did bid us follow to the temple.

DEMETRIUS. Why, then, we are awake; let's follow him;
    And by the way let us recount our dreams.

[Exeunt]

BOTTOM. [Awaking] When my cue comes, call me, and I will answer.
My next is 'Most fair Pyramus.' Heigh-ho! Peter Quince! Flute, the
bellows-mender! Snout, the tinker! Starveling! God's my life, stol'n
hence, and left me asleep! I have had a most rare vision. I have had a
dream, past the wit of man to say what dream it was. Man is but an ass
if he go about to expound this dream. Methought I was- there is no
man can tell what. Methought I was, and methought I had, but man is
but a patch'd fool, if he will offer to say what methought I had. The eye
of man hath not heard, the ear of man hath not seen, man's hand is not
able to taste, his tongue to conceive, nor his heart to report, what my
dream was. I will get Peter Quince to write a ballad of this dream. It
shall be call'd 'Bottom's Dream,' because it hath no bottom; and I will
sing it in the latter end of a play, before the Duke. Peradventure, to
make it the more gracious, I shall sing it at her death.

[Exit]

SCENE II. Athens. QUINCE'S house

[Enter QUINCE, FLUTE, SNOUT, and STARVELING]

QUINCE. Have you sent to Bottom's house? Is he come home yet?

STARVELING. He cannot be heard of. Out of doubt he is
transported.

FLUTE. If he come not, then the play is marr'd; it goes not

forward, doth it?

QUINCE. It is not possible. You have not a man in all Athens able to discharge Pyramus but he.

FLUTE. No; he hath simply the best wit of any handicraft man in Athens.

QUINCE. Yea, and the best person too; and he is a very paramour for a sweet voice.

FLUTE. You must say 'paragon.' A paramour is- God bless us!- A thing of naught.

[Enter SNUG]

SNUG. Masters, the Duke is coming from the temple; and there is or three lords and ladies more married. If our sport had gone forward, we had all been made men.

FLUTE. O sweet bully Bottom! Thus hath he lost sixpence a day during his life; he could not have scaped sixpence a day. An the Duke had not given him sixpence a day for playing Pyramus, I'll be hanged. He would have deserved it: sixpence a day in Pyramus, or nothing.

[Enter BOTTOM]

BOTTOM. Where are these lads? Where are these hearts?

QUINCE. Bottom! O most courageous day! O most happy hour!

BOTTOM. Masters, I am to discourse wonders; but ask me not what; for if I tell you, I am not true Athenian. I will tell you everything, right as it fell out.

QUINCE. Let us hear, sweet Bottom.

BOTTOM. Not a word of me. All that I will tell you is, that the Duke
hath dined. Get your apparel together; good strings to your beards,
new ribbons to your pumps; meet presently at the palace; every man
look o'er his part; for the short and the long is, our play is preferr'd. In
any case, let Thisby have clean linen; and let not him that plays the
lion pare his nails, for they shall hang out for the lion's claws. And,
most dear actors, eat no onions nor garlic, for we are to utter sweet
breath; and I do not doubt but to hear them say it is a sweet comedy.
No more words. Away, go, away!

[Exeunt]

ACT V

ACT V. SCENE I. Athens. The palace of THESEUS

[Enter THESEUS, HIPPOLYTA, PHILOSTRATE, LORDS, and ATTENDANTS]

HIPPOLYTA. 'Tis strange, my Theseus, that these lovers speak of.

THESEUS. More strange than true. I never may believe
   These antique fables, nor these fairy toys.
   Lovers and madmen have such seething brains,
   Such shaping fantasies, that apprehend
   More than cool reason ever comprehends.
   The lunatic, the lover, and the poet,
   Are of imagination all compact.
   One sees more devils than vast hell can hold;
   That is the madman. The lover, all as frantic,
   Sees Helen's beauty in a brow of Egypt.
   The poet's eye, in a fine frenzy rolling,
   Doth glance from heaven to earth, from earth to heaven;

And as imagination bodies forth
The forms of things unknown, the poet's pen
Turns them to shapes, and gives to airy nothing
A local habitation and a name.
Such tricks hath strong imagination
That, if it would but apprehend some joy,
It comprehends some bringer of that joy;
Or in the night, imagining some fear,
How easy is a bush suppos'd a bear?

HIPPOLYTA. But all the story of the night told over,
   And all their minds transfigur'd so together,
   More witnesseth than fancy's images,
   And grows to something of great constancy,
   But howsoever strange and admirable.

   [Enter LYSANDER, DEMETRIUS, HERMIA, and HELENA]

THESEUS. Here come the lovers, full of joy and mirth.
   Joy, gentle friends, joy and fresh days of love
   Accompany your hearts!

LYSANDER. More than to us
   Wait in your royal walks, your board, your bed!

THESEUS. Come now; what masques, what dances shall we have,
   To wear away this long age of three hours
   Between our after-supper and bed-time?
   Where is our usual manager of mirth?
   What revels are in hand? Is there no play
   To ease the anguish of a torturing hour?
   Call Philostrate.

PHILOSTRATE. Here, mighty Theseus.

THESEUS. Say, what abridgment have you for this evening?

What masque? what music? How shall we beguile
The lazy time, if not with some delight?

PHILOSTRATE. There is a brief how many sports are ripe;
Make choice of which your Highness will see first.

[Giving a paper]

THESEUS. 'The battle with the Centaurs, to be sung
By an Athenian eunuch to the harp.'
We'll none of that: that have I told my love,
In glory of my kinsman Hercules.
'The riot of the tipsy Bacchanals,
Tearing the Thracian singer in their rage.'
That is an old device, and it was play'd
When I from Thebes came last a conqueror.
'The thrice three Muses mourning for the death
Of Learning, late deceas'd in beggary.'
That is some satire, keen and critical,
Not sorting with a nuptial ceremony.
'A tedious brief scene of young Pyramus
And his love Thisby; very tragical mirth.'
Merry and tragical! tedious and brief!
That is hot ice and wondrous strange snow.
How shall we find the concord of this discord?

PHILOSTRATE. A play there is, my lord, some ten words long,
Which is as brief as I have known a play;
But by ten words, my lord, it is too long,
Which makes it tedious; for in all the play
There is not one word apt, one player fitted.
And tragical, my noble lord, it is;
For Pyramus therein doth kill himself.
Which when I saw rehears'd, I must confess,
Made mine eyes water; but more merry tears
The passion of loud laughter never shed.

THESEUS. What are they that do play it?

PHILOSTRATE. Hard-handed men that work in Athens here,
   Which never labour'd in their minds till now;
   And now have toil'd their unbreathed memories
   With this same play against your nuptial.

THESEUS. And we will hear it.

PHILOSTRATE. No, my noble lord,
   It is not for you. I have heard it over,
   And it is nothing, nothing in the world;
   Unless you can find sport in their intents,
   Extremely stretch'd and conn'd with cruel pain,
   To do you service.

THESEUS. I will hear that play;
   For never anything can be amiss
   When simpleness and duty tender it.
   Go, bring them in; and take your places, ladies.

                              [Exit PHILOSTRATE]

HIPPOLYTA. I love not to see wretchedness o'er-charged,
   And duty in his service perishing.

THESEUS. Why, gentle sweet, you shall see no such thing.

HIPPOLYTA. He says they can do nothing in this kind.

THESEUS. The kinder we, to give them thanks for nothing.
   Our sport shall be to take what they mistake;
   And what poor duty cannot do, noble respect
   Takes it in might, not merit.
   Where I have come, great clerks have purposed
   To greet me with premeditated welcomes;

Where I have seen them shiver and look pale,
Make periods in the midst of sentences,
Throttle their practis'd accent in their fears,
And, in conclusion, dumbly have broke off,
Not paying me a welcome. Trust me, sweet,
Out of this silence yet I pick'd a welcome;
And in the modesty of fearful duty
I read as much as from the rattling tongue
Of saucy and audacious eloquence.
Love, therefore, and tongue-tied simplicity
In least speak most to my capacity.

[Re-enter PHILOSTRATE]

PHILOSTRATE. SO please your Grace, the Prologue is address'd.

THESEUS. Let him approach.

[Flourish of trumpets]

[Enter QUINCE as the PROLOGUE]

PROLOGUE. If we offend, it is with our good will.
   That you should think, we come not to offend,
   But with good will. To show our simple skill,
   That is the true beginning of our end.
   Consider then, we come but in despite.
   We do not come, as minding to content you,
   Our true intent is. All for your delight
   We are not here. That you should here repent you,
   The actors are at band; and, by their show,
   You shall know all, that you are like to know.

THESEUS. This fellow doth not stand upon points.

LYSANDER. He hath rid his prologue like a rough colt; he knows not

the stop. A good moral, my lord: it is not enough to speak, but
to speak true.

HIPPOLYTA. Indeed he hath play'd on this prologue like a child on a
recorder- a sound, but not in government.

THESEUS. His speech was like a tangled chain; nothing
impaired, but all disordered. Who is next?

[Enter, with a trumpet before them, as in dumb show,
PYRAMUS and THISBY, WALL, MOONSHINE, and LION]

PROLOGUE. Gentles, perchance you wonder at this show;
    But wonder on, till truth make all things plain.
    This man is Pyramus, if you would know;
    This beauteous lady Thisby is certain.
    This man, with lime and rough-cast, doth present
    Wall, that vile Wall which did these lovers sunder;
    And through Walls chink, poor souls, they are content
    To whisper. At the which let no man wonder.
    This man, with lanthorn, dog, and bush of thorn,
    Presenteth Moonshine; for, if you will know,
    By moonshine did these lovers think no scorn
    To meet at Ninus' tomb, there, there to woo.
    This grisly beast, which Lion hight by name,
    The trusty Thisby, coming first by night,
    Did scare away, or rather did affright;
    And as she fled, her mantle she did fall;
    Which Lion vile with bloody mouth did stain.
    Anon comes Pyramus, sweet youth and tall,
    And finds his trusty Thisby's mantle slain;
    Whereat with blade, with bloody blameful blade,
    He bravely broach'd his boiling bloody breast;
    And Thisby, tarrying in mulberry shade,
    His dagger drew, and died. For all the rest,
    Let Lion, Moonshine, Wall, and lovers twain,

At large discourse while here they do remain.

> [Exeunt PROLOGUE, PYRAMUS, THISBY,
> LION, and MOONSHINE]

THESEUS. I wonder if the lion be to speak.

DEMETRIUS. No wonder, my lord: one lion may, when many
asses do.

WALL. In this same interlude it doth befall
  That I, one Snout by name, present a wall;
  And such a wall as I would have you think
  That had in it a crannied hole or chink,
  Through which the lovers, Pyramus and Thisby,
  Did whisper often very secretly.
  This loam, this rough-cast, and this stone, doth show
  That I am that same wall; the truth is so;
  And this the cranny is, right and sinister,
  Through which the fearful lovers are to whisper.

THESEUS. Would you desire lime and hair to speak better?

DEMETRIUS. It is the wittiest partition that ever I heard
  discourse, my lord.

> [Enter PYRAMUS]

THESEUS. Pyramus draws near the wall; silence.

PYRAMUS. O grim-look'd night! O night with hue so black!
  O night, which ever art when day is not!
  O night, O night, alack, alack, alack,
  I fear my Thisby's promise is forgot!
  And thou, O wall, O sweet, O lovely wall,
  That stand'st between her father's ground and mine;

Thou wall, O wall, O sweet and lovely wall,
Show me thy chink, to blink through with mine eyne.
    [WALL holds up his fingers]
Thanks, courteous wall. Jove shield thee well for this!
But what see what see I? No Thisby do I see.
O wicked wall, through whom I see no bliss,
Curs'd be thy stones for thus deceiving me!

THESEUS. The wall, methinks, being sensible, should curse again.

PYRAMUS. No, in truth, sir, he should not. Deceiving me is Thisby's
    cue. She is to enter now, and I am to spy her through the wall.
    You shall see it will fall pat as I told you; yonder she comes.

[Enter THISBY]

THISBY. O wall, full often hast thou beard my moans,
    For parting my fair Pyramus and me!
    My cherry lips have often kiss'd thy stones,
    Thy stones with lime and hair knit up in thee.

PYRAMUS. I see a voice; now will I to the chink,
    To spy an I can hear my Thisby's face.
    Thisby!

THISBY. My love! thou art my love, I think.

PYRAMUS. Think what thou wilt, I am thy lover's grace;
    And like Limander am I trusty still.

THISBY. And I like Helen, till the Fates me kill.

PYRAMUS. Not Shafalus to Procrus was so true.

THISBY. As Shafalus to Procrus, I to you.

PYRAMUS. O, kiss me through the hole of this vile wall.

THISBY. I kiss the wall's hole, not your lips at all.

PYRAMUS. Wilt thou at Ninny's tomb meet me straightway?

THISBY. Tide life, tide death, I come without delay.

[Exeunt PYRAMUS and THISBY]

WALL. Thus have I, Wall, my part discharged so;
   And, being done, thus Wall away doth go.

[Exit WALL]

THESEUS. Now is the moon used between the two neighbours.

DEMETRIUS. No remedy, my lord, when walls are so wilful to hear
   without warning.

HIPPOLYTA. This is the silliest stuff that ever I heard.

THESEUS. The best in this kind are but shadows; and the worst are
   no worse, if imagination amend them.

HIPPOLYTA. It must be your imagination then, and not theirs.

THESEUS. If we imagine no worse of them than they of themselves,
   they may pass for excellent men. Here come two noble beasts in, a
   man and a lion.

[Enter LION and MOONSHINE]

LION. You, ladies, you, whose gentle hearts do fear
   The smallest monstrous mouse that creeps on floor,
   May now, perchance, both quake and tremble here,

When lion rough in wildest rage doth roar.
Then know that I as Snug the joiner am
A lion fell, nor else no lion's dam;
For, if I should as lion come in strife
Into this place, 'twere pity on my life.

THESEUS. A very gentle beast, and of a good conscience.

DEMETRIUS. The very best at a beast, my lord, that e'er I saw.

LYSANDER. This lion is a very fox for his valour.

THESEUS. True; and a goose for his discretion.

DEMETRIUS. Not so, my lord; for his valour cannot carry his
discretion, and the fox carries the goose.

THESEUS. His discretion, I am sure, cannot carry his valour; for
the goose carries not the fox. It is well. Leave it to his
discretion, and let us listen to the Moon.

MOONSHINE. This lanthorn doth the horned moon present-

DEMETRIUS. He should have worn the horns on his head.

THESEUS. He is no crescent, and his horns are invisible within the
circumference.

MOONSHINE. This lanthorn doth the horned moon present;
Myself the Man i' th' Moon do seem to be.

THESEUS. This is the greatest error of all the rest; the man should
be put into the lantern. How is it else the man i' th' moon?

DEMETRIUS. He dares not come there for the candle; for, you see, it
is already in snuff.

HIPPOLYTA. I am aweary of this moon. Would he would change!

THESEUS. It appears, by his small light of discretion, that he is
in the wane; but yet, in courtesy, in all reason, we must stay
the time.

LYSANDER. Proceed, Moon.

MOON. All that I have to say is to tell you that the lanthorn is
the moon; I, the Man i' th' Moon; this thorn-bush, my thorn-bush;
and this dog, my dog.

DEMETRIUS. Why, all these should be in the lantern; for all these
are in the moon. But silence; here comes Thisby.

[Re-enter THISBY]

THISBY. This is old Ninny's tomb. Where is my love?

LION. [Roaring] O-

[THISBY runs off]

DEMETRIUS. Well roar'd, Lion.

THESEUS. Well run, Thisby.

HIPPOLYTA. Well shone, Moon. Truly, the moon shines with a
good grace.

[The LION tears THISBY'S Mantle, and exit]

THESEUS. Well mous'd, Lion.

[Re-enter PYRAMUS]

DEMETRIUS. And then came Pyramus.

LYSANDER. And so the lion vanish'd.

PYRAMUS. Sweet Moon, I thank thee for thy sunny beams;
  I thank thee, Moon, for shining now so bright;
  For, by thy gracious golden, glittering gleams,
  I trust to take of truest Thisby sight.
  But stay, O spite!
  But mark, poor knight,
  What dreadful dole is here!
  Eyes, do you see?
  How can it he?
  O dainty duck! O dear!
  Thy mantle good,
  What! stain'd with blood?
  Approach, ye Furies fell.
  O Fates! come, come;
  Cut thread and thrum;
  Quail, crush, conclude, and quell.

THESEUS. This passion, and the death of a dear friend, would go
  near to make a man look sad.

HIPPOLYTA. Beshrew my heart, but I pity the man.

PYRAMUS. O wherefore, Nature, didst thou lions frame?
  Since lion vile hath here deflower'd my dear;
  Which is- no, no- which was the fairest dame
  That liv'd, that lov'd, that lik'd, that look'd with cheer.
  Come, tears, confound;
  Out, sword, and wound
  The pap of Pyramus;
  Ay, that left pap,
  Where heart doth hop. [Stabs himself]
  Thus die I, thus, thus, thus.

Now am I dead,
Now am I fled;
My soul is in the sky.
Tongue, lose thy light;
Moon, take thy flight. [Exit MOONSHINE]
Now die, die, die, die, die. [Dies]

DEMETRIUS. No die, but an ace, for him; for he is but one.

LYSANDER. Less than an ace, man; for he is dead; he is nothing.

THESEUS. With the help of a surgeon he might yet recover and yet
prove an ass.

HIPPOLYTA. How chance Moonshine is gone before Thisby
comes back
   and finds her lover?

[Re-enter THISBY]

THESEUS. She will find him by starlight. Here she comes; and her
passion ends the play.

HIPPOLYTA. Methinks she should not use a long one for such a
Pyramus; I hope she will be brief.

DEMETRIUS. A mote will turn the balance, which Pyramus, which
Thisby, is the better- he for a man, God warrant us: She for a
woman, God bless us!

LYSANDER. She hath spied him already with those sweet eyes.

DEMETRIUS. And thus she moans, videlicet:-

THISBY. Asleep, my love?
      What, dead, my dove?

O Pyramus, arise,
Speak, speak. Quite dumb?
Dead, dead? A tomb
Must cover thy sweet eyes.
These lily lips,
This cherry nose,
These yellow cowslip cheeks,
Are gone, are gone;
Lovers, make moan;
His eyes were green as leeks.
O Sisters Three,
Come, come to me,
With hands as pale as milk;
Lay them in gore,
Since you have shore
With shears his thread of silk.
Tongue, not a word.
Come, trusty sword;
Come, blade, my breast imbrue. [Stabs herself]
And farewell, friends;
Thus Thisby ends;
Adieu, adieu, adieu. [Dies]

THESEUS. Moonshine and Lion are left to bury the dead.

DEMETRIUS. Ay, and Wall too.

BOTTOM. [Starting up] No, I assure you; the wall is down that parted
their fathers. Will it please you to see the Epilogue, or to hear a Bergomask dance between two of our company?

THESEUS. No epilogue, I pray you; for your play needs no excuse.
Never excuse; for when the players are all dead there need none
to be blamed. Marry, if he that writ it had played Pyramus, and
hang'd himself in Thisby's garter, it would have been a fine
tragedy. And so it is, truly; and very notably discharg'd. But

come, your Bergomask; let your epilogue alone. [A dance]
The iron tongue of midnight hath told twelve.
Lovers, to bed; 'tis almost fairy time.
I fear we shall out-sleep the coming morn,
As much as we this night have overwatch'd.
This palpable-gross play hath well beguil'd
The heavy gait of night. Sweet friends, to bed.
A fortnight hold we this solemnity,
In nightly revels and new jollity.

[Exeunt]

[Enter PUCK with a broom]

PUCK. Now the hungry lion roars,
     And the wolf behowls the moon;
     Whilst the heavy ploughman snores,
     All with weary task fordone.
     Now the wasted brands do glow,
     Whilst the screech-owl, screeching loud,
     Puts the wretch that lies in woe
     In remembrance of a shroud.
     Now it is the time of night
     That the graves, all gaping wide,
     Every one lets forth his sprite,
     In the church-way paths to glide.
     And we fairies, that do run
     By the triple Hecate's team
     From the presence of the sun,
     Following darkness like a dream,
     Now are frolic. Not a mouse
     Shall disturb this hallowed house.
     I am sent with broom before,
     To sweep the dust behind the door.

[Enter OBERON and TITANIA, with all their train]

OBERON. Through the house give glimmering light,
　　　　By the dead and drowsy fire;
　　　　Every elf and fairy sprite
　　　　Hop as light as bird from brier;
　　　　And this ditty, after me,
　　　　Sing and dance it trippingly.

TITANIA. First, rehearse your song by rote,
　　　　To each word a warbling note;
　　　　Hand in hand, with fairy grace,
　　　　Will we sing, and bless this place.

　　　　[OBERON leading, the FAIRIES sing and dance]

OBERON. Now, until the break of day,
　　　　Through this house each fairy stray.
　　　　To the best bride-bed will we,
　　　　Which by us shall blessed be;
　　　　And the issue there create
　　　　Ever shall be fortunate.
　　　　So shall all the couples three
　　　　Ever true in loving be;
　　　　And the blots of Nature's hand
　　　　Shall not in their issue stand;
　　　　Never mole, hare-lip, nor scar,
　　　　Nor mark prodigious, such as are
　　　　Despised in nativity,
　　　　Shall upon their children be.
　　　　With this field-dew consecrate,
　　　　Every fairy take his gait,
　　　　And each several chamber bless,
　　　　Through this palace, with sweet peace;
　　　　And the owner of it blest
　　　　Ever shall in safety rest.
　　　　Trip away; make no stay;
　　　　Meet me all by break of day.

[Exeunt all but PUCK]

PUCK. If we shadows have offended,
  Think but this, and all is mended,
  That you have but slumb'red here
  While these visions did appear.
  And this weak and idle theme,
  No more yielding but a dream,
  Gentles, do not reprehend.
  If you pardon, we will mend.
  And, as I am an honest Puck,
  If we have unearned luck
  Now to scape the serpent's tongue,
  We will make amends ere long;
  Else the Puck a liar call.
  So, good night unto you all.
  Give me your hands, if we be friends,
  And Robin shall restore amends.

[Exit]

THE END

DISCUSSION QUESTIONS

1. Who would you label as the play's protagonist and antagonist?
2. What themes are explored throughout this play?
3. To what extent do the female characters such as Hermia and Helena possess agency—do they control their own fate?
4. In what ways do the pairs of young Athenian lovers (Demetrius and Lysander; Helena and Hermia) mirror each other?
5. What is the significance regarding the shift from iambic pentameter to free verse when going back and forth between the dialogue of the Athenians and that of the acting troupe? (See notable change between Act I, Scene 2 and Act II, Scene 1).
6. How do the Athenian lovers compare to the members of the acting troupe?
7. What is learned about Bottom's character in his attempt to play numerous roles in the acting troupe's production of *The Most Lamentable Comedy and Most Cruel Death of Pyramus and Thisbe*?
8. What do the moon and moonlight symbolize?

9. How does the conflict between Titania and Oberon parallel that of the Athenian lovers?

10. Does Puck mistakenly curse the wrong people, or does he deliberately bewitch them to create humorous chaos? Does he possess an entirely different set of motivations independent from Oberon?

11. For what purpose does the acting troupe amend crucial plot points of the Pyramus and Thisbe story? What is gained and lost by these changes?

12. What is the significance of Bottom's transformation, gaining the head of an ass?

13. To what extent do elements of homoeroticism impact the conflict between Helena and Hermia? (See example in Act III, Scene 2, starting, "We, Hermia, like two artificial gods..."). Does this theme extend to other characters and their relationships?

14. Do you think Titania's fairies are aware that she has been bewitched and fallen in love with an ass? If so, why do they not attempt to dissuade her?

15. Why does Oberon want Titania's Indian boy?

16. How does this play represent love, particularly in its relationship to magic?

17. Why does the acting troupe perform *The Most Lamentable Comedy and Most Cruel Death of Pyramus and Thisbe*, and what does it say about love and romantic tribulations?

18. What is the significance of Puck's concluding soliloquy?

19. How do the prologue to the Pyramus and Thisbe story and Puck's concluding remarks resemble one another?

20. What role does comedy serve throughout the play?

Arthur Rackham Illustration from A Midsummer Night's
Dream

CYRANO DE BERGERAC

Edmond Rostand

Translated from the French by Gladys Thomas and Mary F. Guillemard

BACKGROUND TO CYRANO DE BERGERAC

SAVINIANVS DE CIRANO de Bergerac Nobilis
Gallus ex Icone apud Nobiles D Domin LE BRET
et DE PRADE Amicos ipsius antiquissimos depicto.
ZH, pinxit.   W, delin. et Sculpsit.

Portrait of Savinien de Cyrano de Bergerac

Edmond Rostand was a French poet and playwright notable for his romantic plays such as *Les Romanesques*—later adapted into the longest-running musical of all-time, *The Fantasticks*—and his most famous play, *Cyrano de Bergerac*. Born into a wealthy family on April 1, 1868 in Marseille, France, Rostand obtained an exceptional education throughout his youth in Paris, studying literature, philosophy, and history. His early life of prosperity and comfort helped establish Rostand as a highly cultured and sophisticated member of Parisian society. Throughout his life Rostand wrote 12 plays, from comedic romances to historical epics. Unlike Shakespeare, Rostand's work was both highly respected and enjoyed throughout his life—although the Shakespearean oeuvre has weathered time far better. Unfortunately,

Rostand died on December 2, 1918, falling victim to the flu pandemic that claimed the lives of tens of millions of people throughout the world. In doing so, Rostand left behind a minimum of two unfinished manuscripts and an impressive legacy.

Rostand's plays diverge from the popular literary movement prominent during his life, naturalism—a genre that focuses on depictions realistic in nature. In a theatrical context this means that the setting and performances are grounded in reality rather than succumbing to the flamboyant or flashy theatrical traditions that distinguishes the theater from real life. Rostand is closely associated with neo-romanticism, a movement which rejects such notions of naturalism. It is important to read Rostand's work with this context in mind because it explains why a play like *Cyrano de Bergerac* would have been structured in the way it was, typically staged with elaborate, ornate costumes and lavish sets rather than minimalist alternatives. *Cyrano de Bergerac* is set in France during the 17th century, often referred to as the Baroque period. During this era, opulent architecture, music, and other art forms were expected and enjoyed. By embracing the extravagant and lush elements in *Cyrano de Bergerac*, Rostand is staying true to the era in which the play is set rather than transplanting a 19th century mentality into a 17th century setting.

DRAMATIS PERSONAE

CYRANO DE BERGERAC
CHRISTIAN DE NEUVILLETTE
COUNT DE GUICHE
RAGUENEAU
LE BRET
CARBON DE CASTEL-JALOUX
THE CADETS
LIGNIERE
DE VALVERT
A MARQUIS
SECOND MARQUIS
THIRD MARQUIS
MONTFLEURY
BELLEROSE
JODELET
CUIGY
BRISSAILLE
THE DOORKEEPER
A LACKEY
A SECOND LACKEY

A BORE
A MUSKETEER
ANOTHER
A SPANISH OFFICER
A PORTER
A BURGHER
HIS SON
A PICKPOCKET
A SPECTATOR
A GUARDSMAN
BERTRAND THE FIFER
A MONK
TWO MUSICIANS
THE POETS
THE PASTRY COOKS
ROXANE
SISTER MARTHA
LISE
THE BUFFET-GIRL
MOTHER MARGUERITE
THE DUENNA
SISTER CLAIRE
AN ACTRESS
THE PAGES
THE SHOP-GIRL

The crowd, troopers, burghers (male and female), marquises, muske-
teers, pickpockets, pastry-cooks, poets, Gascons cadets, actors (male
and female), violinists, pages, children, soldiers, Spaniards, spectators
(male and female), precieuses, nuns, etc.

ACT I

A Representation at the Hotel de Bourgogne.

The hall of the Hotel de Bourgogne, in 1640. A sort of tennis-court arranged and decorated for a theatrical performance.

The hall is oblong and seen obliquely, so that one of its sides forms the back of the right foreground, and meeting the left background makes an angle with the stage, which is partly visible.

On both sides of the stage are benches. The curtain is composed of two tapestries which can be drawn aside. Above a harlequin's mantle are the royal arms. There are broad steps from the stage to the hall; on either side of these steps are the places for the violinists. Footlights.

Two rows, one over the other, of side galleries: the highest divided into boxes. No seats in the pit of the hall, which is the real stage of the theater; at the back of the pit, i.e., on the right foreground, some benches forming steps, and underneath, a staircase which leads to the upper seats. An improvised buffet ornamented with little lusters, vases, glasses, plates of tarts, cakes, bottles, etc.

The entrance to the theater is in the center of the background, under the gallery of the boxes. A large door, half open to let in the spectators. On the panels of this door, in different corners, and over the buffet, red placards bearing the words, 'La Clorise.'

At the rising of the curtain the hall is in semi-darkness, and still empty. The lusters are lowered in the middle of the pit ready to be lighted.

Act I. Scene I.

The public, arriving by degrees. Troopers, burghers, lackeys, pages, a pickpocket, the doorkeeper, etc., followed by the marquises. Cuigy, Brissaille, the buffet-girl, the violinists, etc.

[A confusion of loud voices is heard outside the door. A trooper enters hastily.]

THE DOORKEEPER [following him].
Hollo! You there! Your money!

THE TROOPER.
I enter gratis.

THE DOORKEEPER.
Why?

THE TROOPER.
Why? I am of the King's Household Cavalry, 'faith!

THE DOORKEEPER [to another trooper who enters].
And you?

SECOND TROOPER.
I pay nothing.

THE DOORKEEPER.
How so?

SECOND TROOPER.
I am a musketeer.

FIRST TROOPER [to the second].
The play will not begin till two. The pit is empty.
Come, a bout with the foils to pass the time.

[They fence with the foils they have brought.]

A LACKEY [entering].
Pst. . .Flanquin. . .!

ANOTHER [already there].
Champagne?. . .

THE FIRST [showing him cards and dice which he takes from his doublet].
See, here be cards and dice.
[He seats himself on the floor]
Let's play.

THE SECOND [doing the same].
Good; I am with you, villain!

FIRST LACKEY [taking from his pocket a candle-end, which he lights, and sticks on the floor].
I made free to provide myself with light at my master's expense!

A GUARDSMAN [to a shop-girl who advances].
'Twas prettily done to come before the lights were lit!

[He takes her round the waist.]

ONE OF THE FENCERS [receiving a thrust].
A hit!

ONE OF THE CARD-PLAYERS.
Clubs!

THE GUARDSMAN [following the girl].
A kiss!

THE SHOP-GIRL [struggling to free herself].
They're looking!

THE GUARDSMAN [drawing her to a dark corner].
No fear! No one can see!

A MAN [sitting on the ground with others, who have brought their
provisions].
By coming early, one can eat in comfort.

A BURGHER [conducting his son].
Let us sit here, son.

A CARD-PLAYER.
Triple ace!

A MAN [taking a bottle from under his cloak,
and also seating himself on the floor].
A tippler may well quaff his Burgundy
[he drinks]
in the Burgundy Hotel!

THE BURGHER [to his son].
'Faith! A man might think he had fallen in a bad house here!
[He points with his cane to the drunkard]
What with topers!
[One of the fencers in breaking off, jostles him.]

Brawlers!
[He stumbles into the midst of the card-players.]
Gamblers!

THE GUARDSMAN [behind him, still teasing the shop-girl].
Come, one kiss!

THE BURGHER [hurriedly pulling his son away].
By all the holies! And this, my boy, is the theater where they played
Rotrou erewhile.

THE YOUNG MAN.
Ay, and Corneille!

A TROOP OF PAGES [hand-in-hand, enter dancing the farandole,
and singing].
Tra' a la, la, la, la, la, la, la, lere. . .

THE DOORKEEPER [sternly, to the pages].
You pages there, none of your tricks!. . .

FIRST PAGE [with an air of wounded dignity].
Oh, sir!--such a suspicion!. . .
[Briskly, to the second page, the moment the doorkeeper's back is
turned]
Have you string?

THE SECOND.
Ay, and a fish-hook with it.

FIRST PAGE.
We can angle for wigs, then, up there i' th' gallery.

A PICKPOCKET [gathering about him some evil-looking youths].
Hark ye, young cut-purses, lend an ear, while I give you your first
lesson in thieving.

SECOND PAGE [calling up to others in the top galleries].
You there! Have you peashooters?

THIRD PAGE [from above].
Ay, have we, and peas withal!

[He blows, and peppers them with peas.]

THE YOUNG MAN [to his father].
What piece do they give us?

THE BURGHER.
'Clorise.'

THE YOUNG MAN.
Who may the author be?

THE BURGHER.
Master Balthazar Baro. It is a play!. . .

[He goes arm-in-arm with his son.]

THE PICKPOCKET [to his pupils].
Have a care, above all, of the lace knee-ruffles--cut them off!

A SPECTATOR [to another, showing him a corner in the gallery].
I was up there, the first night of the 'Cid.'

THE PICKPOCKET [making with his fingers the gesture of filching].
Thus for watches--

THE BURGHER [coming down again with his son].
Ah! You shall presently see some renowned actors. . .

THE PICKPOCKET [making the gestures of one who pulls something stealthily, with little jerks].

Thus for handkerchiefs--

THE BURGHER.
Montfleury. . .

SOME ONE [shouting from the upper gallery].
Light up, below there!

THE BURGHER.
. . .Bellerose, L'Epy, La Beaupre, Jodelet!

A PAGE [in the pit].
Here comes the buffet-girl!

THE BUFFET-GIRL [taking her place behind the buffet].
Oranges, milk, raspberry-water, cedar bitters!

[A hubbub outside the door is heard.]

A FALSETTO VOICE.
Make place, brutes!

A LACKEY [astonished].
The Marquises!--in the pit?. . .

ANOTHER LACKEY.
Oh! only for a minute or two!

[Enter a band of young marquises.]

A MARQUIS [seeing that the hall is half empty].
What now! So we make our entrance like a pack of woolen-drapers!
Peaceably, without disturbing the folk, or treading on their toes!-
-Oh, fie!
Fie!

[Recognizing some other gentlemen who have entered a little before him]
Cuigy! Brissaille!

[Greetings and embraces.]

CUIGY.
True to our word!. . .Troth, we are here before the candles are lit.

THE MARQUIS.
Ay, indeed! Enough! I am of an ill humor.

ANOTHER.
Nay, nay, Marquis! see, for your consolation, they are coming to light up!

ALL THE AUDIENCE [welcoming the entrance of the lighter].
Ah!. . .

[They form in groups round the lusters as they are lit. Some people have taken their seats in the galleries. Ligniere, a distinguished-looking roue, with disordered shirt-front arm-in-arm with christian de Neuvillette. Christian, who is dressed elegantly, but rather behind the fashion, seems preoccupied, and keeps looking at the boxes.]

Act I. Scene II.

[The same. Christian, Ligniere, then Ragueneau and Le Bret.]

CUIGY.
Ligniere!

BRISSAILLE [laughing].
Not drunk as yet?

LIGNIERE [aside to Christian].

I may introduce you?
[Christian nods in assent]
Baron de Neuvillette.

[Bows.]

THE AUDIENCE [applauding as the first luster is lighted and drawn up].
Ah!

CUIGY [to Brissaille, looking at Christian].
'Tis a pretty fellow!

FIRST MARQUIS [who has overheard].
Pooh!

LIGNIERE [introducing them to Christian].
My lords De Cuigy. De Brissaille. . .

CHRISTIAN [bowing].
Delighted!. . .

FIRST MARQUIS [to second].
He is not ill to look at, but certes, he is not costumed in the latest mode.

LIGNIERE [to Cuigy].
This gentleman comes from Touraine.

CHRISTIAN.
Yes, I have scarce been twenty days in Paris; tomorrow I join the Guards, in the Cadets.

FIRST MARQUIS [watching the people who are coming into the boxes].
There is the wife of the Chief-Justice.

THE BUFFET-GIRL.
Oranges, milk. . .

THE VIOLINISTS [tuning up].
La--la--

CUIGY [to Christian, pointing to the hall, which is filling fast].
'Tis crowded.

CHRISTIAN.
Yes, indeed.

FIRST MARQUIS.
All the great world!

[They recognize and name the different elegantly dressed ladies who
enter the boxes, bowing low to them. The ladies send smiles in
answer.]

SECOND MARQUIS.
Madame de Guemenee.

CUIGY.
Madame de Bois-Dauphin.

FIRST MARQUIS.
Adored by us all!

BRISSAILLE.
Madame de Chavigny. . .

SECOND MARQUIS.
Who sports with our poor hearts!. . .

LIGNIERE.
Ha! so Monsieur de Corneille has come back from Rouen!

THE YOUNG MAN [to his father].
Is the Academy here?

THE BURGHER.
Oh, ay, I see several of them. There is Boudu, Boissat,
and Cureau de la Chambre, Porcheres, Colomby, Bourzeys,
Bourdon, Arbaud. . .all names that will live! 'Tis fine!

FIRST MARQUIS.
Attention! Here come our precieuses; Barthenoide, Urimedonte,
Cassandace, Felixerie. . .

SECOND MARQUIS.
Ah! How exquisite their fancy names are! Do you know them all,
Marquis?

FIRST MARQUIS.
Ay, Marquis, I do, every one!

LIGNIERE [drawing Christian aside].
Friend, I but came here to give you pleasure. The lady comes not. I will
betake me again to my pet vice.

CHRISTIAN [persuasively].
No, no! You, who are ballad-maker to Court and City alike, can tell me
better than any who the lady is for whom I die of love. Stay yet awhile.

THE FIRST VIOLIN [striking his bow on the desk].
Gentlemen violinists!

[He raises his bow.]

THE BUFFET-GIRL.
Macaroons, lemon-drink. . .

[The violins begin to play.]

CHRISTIAN.
Ah! I fear me she is coquettish, and over nice and fastidious!
I, who am so poor of wit, how dare I speak to her--how address her?
This language that they speak to-day--ay, and write--confounds me;
I am but an honest soldier, and timid withal. She has ever her place,
there, on the right--the empty box, see you!

LIGNIERE [making as if to go].
I must go.

CHRISTIAN [detaining him].
Nay, stay.

LIGNIERE.
I cannot. D'Assoucy waits me at the tavern, and here one dies of
thirst.

THE BUFFET-GIRL [passing before him with a tray].
Orange drink?

LIGNIERE.
Ugh!

THE BUFFET-GIRL.
Milk?

LIGNIERE.
Pah!

THE BUFFET-GIRL.
Rivesalte?

LIGNIERE.
Stay.
[To Christian]
I will remain awhile.--Let me taste this rivesalte.

[He sits by the buffet; the girl pours some out for him.]

CRIES [from all the audience, at the entrance of a plump little man, joyously excited].
Ah! Ragueneau!

LIGNIERE [to Christian].
'Tis the famous tavern-keeper Ragueneau.

RAGUENEAU [dressed in the Sunday clothes of a pastry-cook, going up quickly to Ligniere].
Sir, have you seen Monsieur de Cyrano?

LIGNIERE [introducing him to Christian].
The pastry-cook of the actors and the poets!

RAGUENEAU [overcome].
You do me too great honor. . .

LIGNIERE.
Nay, hold your peace, Maecenas that you are!

RAGUENEAU.
True, these gentlemen employ me. . .

LIGNIERE.
On credit!
He is himself a poet of a pretty talent. . .

RAGUENEAU.
So they tell me.

LIGNIERE.
--Mad after poetry!

RAGUENEAU.

'Tis true that, for a little ode. . .

LIGNIERE.
You give a tart. . .

RAGUENEAU.
Oh!--a tartlet!

LIGNIERE.
Brave fellow! He would fain fain excuse himself!
--And for a triolet, now, did you not give in exchange. . .

RAGUENEAU.
Some little rolls!

LIGNIERE [severely].
They were milk-rolls! And as for the theater, which you love?

RAGUENEAU.
Oh! to distraction!

LIGNIERE.
How pay you your tickets, ha?--with cakes.
Your place, to-night, come tell me in my ear, what did it cost you?

RAGUENEAU.
Four custards, and fifteen cream-puffs.
[He looks around on all sides]
Monsieur de Cyrano is not here? 'Tis strange.

LIGNIERE.
Why so?

RAGUENEAU.
Montfleury plays!

LIGNIERE.
Ay, 'tis true that that old wine-barrel is to take Phedon's part to-night;
but what matter is that to Cyrano?

RAGUENEAU.
How? Know you not? He has got a hot hate for Montfleury, and
so!--has
forbid him strictly to show his face on the stage for one whole month.

LIGNIERE [drinking his fourth glass].
Well?

RAGUENEAU.
Montfleury will play!

CUIGY.
He can not hinder that.

RAGUENEAU.
Oh! oh! that I have come to see!

FIRST MARQUIS.
Who is this Cyrano?

CUIGY.
A fellow well skilled in all tricks of fence.

SECOND MARQUIS.
Is he of noble birth?

CUIGY.
Ay, noble enough. He is a cadet in the Guards.
[Pointing to a gentleman who is going up and down the hall as if
searching for some one]
But 'tis his friend Le Bret, yonder, who can best tell you.
[He calls him]

Le Bret!
[Le Bret comes towards them]
Seek you for De Bergerac?

LE BRET.
Ay, I am uneasy. . .

CUIGY.
Is it not true that he is the strangest of men?

LE BRET [tenderly].
True, that he is the choicest of earthly beings!

RAGUENEAU.
Poet!

CUIGY.
Soldier!

BRISSAILLE.
Philosopher!

LE BRET.
Musician!

LIGNIERE.
And of how fantastic a presence!

RAGENEAU.
Marry, 'twould puzzle even our grim painter Philippe de Champaigne
to portray him! Methinks, whimsical, wild, comical as he is, only
Jacques Callot, now dead and gone, had succeeded better, and had
made of him the maddest fighter of all his visored crew--with his
triple-plumed beaver and six-pointed doublet--the sword-point
sticking up 'neath his mantle like an insolent cocktail! He's prouder
than all the fierce Artabans of whom Gascony has ever been and will

ever be the prolific Alma Mater! Above his Toby ruff he carries a nose!-
-ah, good my lords, what a nose is his! When one sees it one is fain to
cry aloud, 'Nay! 'tis too much! He plays a joke on us!' Then one laughs,
says 'He will anon take it off.' But no!--Monsieur de Bergerac always
keeps it on.

LE BRET [throwing back his head].
He keeps it on--and cleaves in two any man who dares remark on it!

RAGUENEAU [proudly].
His sword--'tis one half of the Fates' shears!

FIRST MARQUIS [shrugging his shoulders].
He will not come!

RAGUENEAU.
I say he will! and I wager a fowl--a la Ragueneau.

THE MARQUIS [laughing].
Good!

[Murmurs of admiration in hall. Roxane has just appeared in her box.
She seats herself in front, the duenna at the back. Christian, who is
paying the buffet-girl, does not see her entrance.]

SECOND MARQUIS [with little cries of joy].
Ah, gentlemen! she is fearfully--terribly--ravishing!

FIRST MARQUIS.
When one looks at her one thinks of a peach smiling at a
strawberry!

SECOND MARQUIS.
And what freshness! A man approaching her too near might chance to
get a bad chill at the heart!

CHRISTIAN [raising his head, sees Roxane, and catches Ligniere by the arm].
'Tis she!

LIGNIERE.
Ah! is it she?

CHRISTIAN.
Ay, tell me quick--I am afraid.

LIGNIERE [tasting his rivesalte in sips].
Magdaleine Robin--Roxane, so called! A subtle wit--a precieuse.

CHRISTIAN.
Woe is me!

LIGNIERE.
Free. An orphan. The cousin of Cyrano, of whom we were now speaking.

   [At this moment an elegant nobleman, with blue ribbon across his
      breast, enters the box, and talks with Roxane, standing.]

CHRISTIAN [starting].
Who is yonder man?

LIGNIERE [who is becoming tipsy, winking at him].
Ha! ha! Count de Guiche. Enamored of her. But wedded to the niece of Armand de Richelieu. Would fain marry Roxane to a certain sorry fellow, one Monsieur de Valvert, a viscount--and--accommodating! She will none of that bargain; but De Guiche is powerful, and can perse-cute the daughter of a plain untitled gentleman. More by token, I myself have exposed this cunning plan of his to the world, in a song which. . .Ho! he must rage at me! The end hit home. . .Listen!

   [He gets up staggering, and raises his glass, ready to sing.]

CHRISTIAN.
No. Good-night.

LIGNIERE.
Where go you?

CHRISTIAN.
To Monsieur de Valvert!

LIGNIERE.
Have a care! It is he who will kill you
[showing him Roxane by a look]
Stay where you are--she is looking at you.

CHRISTIAN.
It is true!

[He stands looking at her. The group of pickpockets seeing him thus,
head in air and open-mouthed, draw near to him.]

LIGNIERE.
'Tis I who am going. I am athirst! And they expect me--in the taverns!

[He goes out, reeling.]

LE BRET [who has been all round the hall, coming back to Ragueneau
reassured].
No sign of Cyrano.

RAGUENEAU [incredulously].
All the same. . .

LE BRET.
A hope is left to me--that he has not seen the playbill!

THE AUDIENCE.

Begin, begin!

Act I. Scene III.

[The same, all but Ligniere. De Guiche, Valvert, then Montfleury.]

A MARQUIS [watching De Guiche, who comes down from Roxane's box, and crosses the pit surrounded by obsequious noblemen, among them the Viscount de Valvert].
He pays a fine court, your De Guiche!

ANOTHER.
Faugh!. . .Another Gascon!

THE FIRST.
Ay, but the cold, supple Gascon—that is the stuff success is made of! Believe me, we had best make our bow to him.

[They go toward De Guiche.]

SECOND MARQUIS.
What fine ribbons! How call you the color, Count de Guiche? 'Kiss me, my darling,' or 'Timid Fawn?'

DE GUICHE.
'Tis the color called 'Sick Spaniard.'

FIRST MARQUIS.
'Faith! The color speaks truth, for, thanks to your valor, things will soon go ill for Spain in Flanders.

DE GUICHE.
I go on the stage! Will you come?
[He goes toward the stage, followed by the marquises and gentlemen. Turning, he calls]
Come you Valvert!

CHRISTIAN [who is watching and listening, starts on hearing this name].
The Viscount! Ah! I will throw full in his face my. . .
[He puts his hand in his pocket, and finds there the hand of a pick-pocket who is about to rob him. He turns round]
Hey?

THE PICKPOCKET.
Oh!

CHRISTIAN [holding him tightly].
I was looking for a glove.

THE PICKPOCKET [smiling piteously].
And you find a hand.
[Changing his tone, quickly and in a whisper]
Let me but go, and I will deliver you a secret.

CHRISTIAN [still holding him].
What is it?

THE PICKPOCKET.
Ligniere. . .he who has just left you. . .

CHRISTIAN [same play].
Well?

THE PICKPOCKET.
His life is in peril. A song writ by him has given offense in high places--and a hundred men--I am of them--are posted to-night. . .

CHRISTIAN.
A hundred men! By whom posted?

THE PICKPOCKET.
I may not say--a secret. . .

CHRISTIAN [shrugging his shoulders].
Oh!

THE PICKPOCKET [with great dignity].
. . .Of the profession.

CHRISTIAN.
Where are they posted?

THE PICKPOCKET.
At the Porte de Nesle. On his way homeward. Warn him.

CHRISTIAN [letting go of his wrists].
But where can I find him?

THE PICKPOCKET.
Run round to all the taverns--The Golden Wine Press, the Pine
Cone, The Belt that Bursts, The Two Torches, The Three
Funnels, and at each leave a word that shall put him on
his guard.

CHRISTIAN.
Good--I fly! Ah, the scoundrels! A hundred men 'gainst one!
[Looking lovingly at Roxane]
Ah, to leave her!. . .
[looking with rage at Valvert]
and him!. . .But save Ligniere I must!

[He hurries out. De Guiche, the viscount, the marquises, have all
disappeared behind the curtain to take their places on the benches
placed on the stage. The pit is quite full; the galleries and boxes are
also crowded.]

THE AUDIENCE.
Begin!

A BURGHER [whose wig is drawn up on the end of a string by a page in the upper gallery].
My wig!

CRIES OF DELIGHT.
He is bald! Bravo, pages--ha! ha! ha!. . .

THE BURGHER [furious, shaking his fist].
Young villain!

LAUGHTER AND CRIES [beginning very loud, and dying gradually away].
Ha! ha! ha! ha! ha! ha!

[Total silence.]

LE BRET [astonished].
What means this sudden silence?. . .
[A spectator says something to him in a low voice]
Is't true?

THE SPECTATOR.
I have just heard it on good authority.

MURMURS [spreading through the hall].
Hush! Is it he? No! Ay, I say!
In the box with the bars in front!
The Cardinal! The Cardinal! The Cardinal!

A PAGE.
The devil! We shall have to behave ourselves. . .

[A knock is heard upon the stage. Every one is motionless. A pause.]

THE VOICE OF A MARQUIS [in the silence, behind the curtain].
Snuff that candle!

ANOTHER MARQUIS [putting his head through the opening in the curtain].
A chair!

[A chair is passed from hand to hand, over the heads of the spectators. The marquis takes it and disappears, after blowing some kisses to the boxes.]

A SPECTATOR.
Silence!

[Three knocks are heard on the stage. The curtain opens in the centre Tableau. The marquises in insolent attitudes seated on each side of the stage. The scene represents a pastoral landscape. Four little lusters light the stage; the violins play softly.]

LE BRET [in a low voice to Ragueneau].
Montfleury comes on the scene?

RAGUENEAU [also in a low voice].
Ay, 'tis he who begins.

LE BRET.
Cyrano is not here.

RAGUENEAU.
I have lost my wager.

LE BRET.
'Tis all the better!

[An air on the drone-pipes is heard, and Montfleury enters, enormously stout, in an Arcadian shepherd's dress, a hat wreathed with roses drooping over one ear, blowing into a ribboned drone pipe.]

THE PIT [applauding].

Bravo, Montfleury! Montfleury!

MONTFLEURY [after bowing low, begins the part of Phedon].
'Heureux qui loin des cours, dans un lieu solitaire,
Se prescrit a soi-meme un exil volontaire,
Et qui, lorsque Zephire a souffle sur les bois. . .'

A VOICE [from the middle of the pit].
Villain! Did I not forbid you to show your face here for month?

[General stupor. Every one turns round. Murmurs.]

DIFFERENT VOICES.
Hey?--What?--What is't?. . .

[The people stand up in the boxes to look.]

CUIGY.
'Tis he!

LE BRET [terrified].
Cyrano!

THE VOICE.
King of clowns! Leave the stage this instant!

ALL THE AUDIENCE [indignantly].
Oh!

MONTFLEURY.
But. . .

THE VOICE.
Do you dare defy me?

DIFFERENT VOICES [from the pit and the boxes].

Peace! Enough!--Play on, Montfleury--fear nothing!

MONTFLEURY [in a trembling voice].
'Heureux qui loin des cours, dans un lieu sol--'

THE VOICE [more fiercely].
Well! Chief of all the blackguards, must I come and give you a taste of my cane?

[A hand holding a cane starts up over the heads of the spectators.]

MONTFLEURY [in a voice that trembles more and more].
'Heureux qui. . .'

[The cane is shaken.]

THE VOICE.
Off the stage!

THE PIT.
Oh!

MONTFLEURY [choking].
'Heureux qui loin des cours. . .'

CYRANO [appearing suddenly in the pit, standing on a chair, his arms crossed, his beaver cocked fiercely, his mustache bristling, his nose terrible to see].
Ah! I shall be angry in a minute!. . .

[Sensation.]

Act I. Scene IV.

[The same. Cyrano, then Bellerose, Jodelet.]

MONTFLEURY [to the marquises].
Come to my help, my lords!

A MARQUIS [carelessly].
Go on! Go on!

CYRANO.
Fat man, take warning! If you go on, I
Shall feel myself constrained to cuff your face!

THE MARQUIS.
Have done!

CYRANO.
And if these lords hold not their tongue
Shall feel constrained to make them taste my cane!

ALL THE MARQUISES [rising].
Enough!. . .Montfleury. . .

CYRANO.
If he goes not quick
I will cut off his ears and slit him up!

A VOICE.
But. . .

CYRANO.
Out he goes!

ANOTHER VOICE.
Yet. . .

CYRANO.
Is he not gone yet?
[He makes the gesture of turning up his cuffs]

Good! I shall mount the stage now, buffet-wise,
To carve this fine Italian sausage--thus!

MONTFLEURY [trying to be dignified].
You outrage Thalia in insulting me!

CYRANO [very politely].
If that Muse, Sir, who knows you not at all,
Could claim acquaintance with you--oh, believe
[Seeing how urn-like, fat, and slow you are]
That she would make you taste her buskin's sole!

THE PIT.
Montfleury! Montfleury! Come--Baro's play!

CYRANO [to those who are calling out].
I pray you have a care! If you go on
My scabbard soon will render up its blade!

[The circle round him widens.]

THE CROWD [drawing back].
Take care!

CYRANO [to Montfleury].
Leave the stage!

THE CROWD [coming near and grumbling].
Oh!--

CYRANO.
Did some one speak?

[They draw back again.]

A VOICE [singing at the back].

Monsieur de Cyrano
Displays his tyrannies:
A fig for tyrants! What, ho!
Come! Play us 'La Clorise!'

ALL THE PIT [singing].
'La Clorise!' 'La Clorise!'. . .

CYRANO.
Let me but hear once more that foolish rhyme,
I slaughter every man of you.

A BURGHER.
Oh! Samson?

CYRANO.
Yes Samson! Will you lend your jawbone, Sir?

A LADY [in the boxes].
Outrageous!

A LORD.
Scandalous!

A BURGHER.
'Tis most annoying!

A PAGE.
Fair good sport!

THE PIT.
Kss!--Montfleury. . .Cyrano!

CYRANO.
Silence!

THE PIT [wildly excited].
Ho-o-o-o-h! Quack! Cock-a-doodle-doo!

CYRANO.
I order--

A PAGE.
Miow!

CYRANO.
I order silence, all!
And challenge the whole pit collectively!--
I write your names!--Approach, young heroes, here!
Each in his turn! I cry the numbers out!--
Now which of you will come to ope the lists?
You, Sir? No! You? No! The first duellist
Shall be dispatched by me with honors due!
Let all who long for death hold up their hands!
[A silence]
Modest? You fear to see my naked blade?
Not one name?--Not one hand?--Good, I proceed!
[Turning toward the stage, where Montfleury waits in an agony]
The theater's too full, congested,--I
Would clear it out. . .If not. . .
[Puts his hand on his sword]
The knife must act!

MONTFLEURY.
I. . .

CYRANO [leaves his chair, and settles himself in the middle of the
circle which has formed].
I will clap my hands thrice, thus--full moon! At the third clap, eclipse
yourself!

THE PIT [amused].

Ah!

CYRANO [clapping his hands].
One!

MONTFLEURY.
I. . .

A VOICE [in the boxes].
Stay!

THE PIT.
He stays. . .he goes. . .he stays. . .

MONTFLEURY.
I think. . .Gentlemen,. . .

CYRANO.
Two!

MONTFLEURY.
I think 'twere wisest. . .

CYRANO.
Three!

[Montfleury disappears as through a trap. Tempest of laughs, whistling
cries, etc.]

THE WHOLE HOUSE.
Coward. . .come back!

CYRANO [delighted, sits back in his chair, arms crossed].
Come back an if you dare!

A BURGHER.

Call for the orator!

[Bellerose comes forward and bows.]

THE BOXES.
Ah! here's Bellerose!

BELLEROSE [elegantly].
My noble lords. . .

THE PIT.
No! no! Jodelet!

JODELET [advancing, speaking through his nose].
Calves!

THE PIT.
Ah! bravo! good! go on!

JODELET.
No bravos, Sirs!
The fat tragedian whom you all love
Felt. . .

THE PIT.
Coward!

JODELET.
. . .was obliged to go.

THE PIT.
Come back!

SOME.
No!

OTHERS.
Yes!

A YOUNG MAN [to Cyrano].
But pray, Sir, for what reason, say,
Hate you Montfleury?

CYRANO [graciously, still seated].
Youthful gander, know
I have two reasons--either will suffice.
Primo. An actor villainous! who mouths,
And heaves up like a bucket from a well
The verses that should, bird-like, fly! Secundo--
That is my secret. . .

THE OLD BURGHER [behind him].
Shameful! You deprive us
Of the 'Clorise!' I must insist. . .

CYRANO [turning his chair toward the burgher, respectfully].
Old mule!
The verses of old Baro are not worth
A doit! I'm glad to interrupt. . .

THE PRECIEUSES [in the boxes].
Our Baro!--
My dear! How dares he venture!. . .

CYRANO [turning his chair toward the boxes gallantly].
Fairest ones,
Radiate, bloom, hold to our lips the cup
Of dreams intoxicating, Hebe-like!
Or, when death strikes, charm death with your sweet smiles;
Inspire our verse, but--criticise it not!

BELLEROSE.

We must give back the entrance fees!

CYRANO [turning his chair toward the stage].
Bellerose,
You make the first intelligent remark!
Would I rend Thespis' sacred mantle? Nay!
[He rises and throws a bag on the stage.]
Catch then the purse I throw, and hold your peace!

THE HOUSE [dazzled].
Ah! Oh!

JODELET [catching the purse dexterously and weighing it].
At this price, you've authority
To come each night, and stop 'Clorise,' Sir!

THE PIT.
Ho!. . .Ho! Ho!. . .

JODELET.
E'en if you chase us in a pack!. . .

BELLEROSE.
Clear out the hall!. . .

JODELET.
Get you all gone at once!

[The people begin to go out, while Cyrano looks on with satisfaction.
  But the crowd soon stop on hearing the following scene, and remain
  where they are. The women, who, with their mantles on, are already
  standing up in the boxes, stop to listen, and finally reseat themselves.]

LE BRET [to Cyrano].
'Tis mad!. . .

A BORE [coming up to Cyrano].
The actor Montfleury! 'Tis shameful!
Why, he's protected by the Duke of Candal!
Have you a patron?

CYRANO.
No!

THE BORE.
No patron?. . .

CYRANO.
None!

THE BORE.
What! no great lord to shield you with his name?

CYRANO [irritated].
No, I have told you twice! Must I repeat?
No! no protector. . .
[His hand on his sword].
A protectress. . .here!

THE BORE.
But you must leave the town?

CYRANO.
Well, that depends!

THE BORE.
The Duke has a long arm!

CYRANO.
But not so long
As mine, when it is lengthened out. . .
[Shows his sword].

As thus!

THE BORE.
You think not to contend?

CYRANO.
'Tis my idea!

THE BORE.
But. . .

CYRANO.
Show your heels! now!

THE BORE.
But I. . .

CYRANO.
Or tell me why you stare so at my nose!

THE BORE [staggered].
I. . .

CYRANO [walking straight up to him].
Well, what is there strange?

THE BORE [drawing back].
Your Grace mistakes!

CYRANO.
How now? Is't soft and dangling, like a trunk?. . .

THE BORE [same play].
I never. . .

CYRANO.

Is it crook'd, like an owl's beak?

THE BORE.
I. . .

CYRANO.
Do you see a wart upon the tip?

THE BORE.
Nay. . .

CYRANO.
Or a fly, that takes the air there? What
Is there to stare at?

THE BORE.
Oh. . .

CYRANO.
What do you see?

THE BORE.
But I was careful not to look--knew better.

CYRANO.
And why not look at it, an if you please?

THE BORE.
I was. . .

CYRANO.
Oh! it disgusts you!

THE BORE.
Sir!

CYRANO.
Its hue
Unwholesome seems to you?

THE BORE.
Sir!

CYRANO.
Or its shape?

THE BORE.
No, on the contrary!. . .

CYRANO.
Why then that air
Disparaging?--perchance you think it large?

THE BORE [stammering].
No, small, quite small--minute!

CYRANO.
Minute! What now?
Accuse me of a thing ridiculous!
Small--my nose?

THE BORE.
Heaven help me!

CYRANO.
'Tis enormous!
Old Flathead, empty-headed meddler, know
That I am proud possessing such appendice.
'Tis well known, a big nose is indicative
Of a soul affable, and kind, and courteous,
Liberal, brave, just like myself, and such
As you can never dare to dream yourself,

Rascal contemptible! For that witless face
That my hand soon will come to cuff--is all
As empty. . .

[He cuffs him.]

THE BORE.
Aie!

CYRANO.
--of pride, of aspiration,
Of feeling, poetry--of godlike spark
Of all that appertains to my big nose,
[He turns him by the shoulders, suiting the action to the word.]
As. . .what my boot will shortly come and kick!

THE BORE [running away].
Help! Call the Guard!

CYRANO.
Take notice, boobies all,
Who find my visage's center ornament
A thing to jest at--that it is my wont--
An if the jester's noble--ere we part
To let him taste my steel, and not my boot!

DE GUICHE [who, with the marquises, has come down from
the stage].
But he becomes a nuisance!

THE VISCOUNT DE VALVERT [shrugging his shoulders].
Swaggerer!

DE GUICHE.
Will no one put him down?. . .

THE VISCOUNT.
No one? But wait!
I'll treat him to. . .one of my quips!. . .See here!. . .
[He goes up to Cyrano, who is watching him, and with a conceited air.]
Sir, your nose is. . .hmm. . .it is. . .very big!

CYRANO [gravely].
Very!

THE VISCOUNT [laughing].
Ha!

CYRANO [imperturbably].
Is that all?. . .

THE VISCOUNT.
What do you mean?

CYRANO.
Ah no! young blade! That was a trifle short!
You might have said at least a hundred things
By varying the tone. . .like this, suppose,. . .
Aggressive: 'Sir, if I had such a nose
I'd amputate it!' Friendly: 'When you sup
It must annoy you, dipping in your cup;
You need a drinking-bowl of special shape!'
Descriptive: ''Tis a rock!. . .a peak!. . .a cape!
--A cape, forsooth! 'Tis a peninsular!'
Curious: 'How serves that oblong capsular?
For scissor-sheath? Or pot to hold your ink?'
Gracious: 'You love the little birds, I think?
I see you've managed with a fond research
To find their tiny claws a roomy perch!'
Truculent: 'When you smoke your pipe. . .suppose
That the tobacco-smoke spouts from your nose--
Do not the neighbors, as the fumes rise higher,

Cry terror-struck: "The chimney is afire"?'
Considerate: 'Take care,. . .your head bowed low
By such a weight. . .lest head o'er heels you go!'
Tender: 'Pray get a small umbrella made,
Lest its bright color in the sun should fade!'
Pedantic: 'That beast Aristophanes
Names Hippocamelelephantoles
Must have possessed just such a solid lump
Of flesh and bone, beneath his forehead's bump!'
Cavalier: 'The last fashion, friend, that hook?
To hang your hat on? 'Tis a useful crook!'
Emphatic: 'No wind, O majestic nose,
Can give THEE cold!--save when the mistral blows!'
Dramatic: 'When it bleeds, what a Red Sea!'
Admiring: 'Sign for a perfumery!'
Lyric: 'Is this a conch?. . .a Triton you?'
Simple: 'When is the monument on view?'
Rustic: 'That thing a nose? Marry-come-up!
'Tis a dwarf pumpkin, or a prize turnip!'
Military: 'Point against cavalry!'
Practical: 'Put it in a lottery!
Assuredly 'twould be the biggest prize!'
Or. . .parodying Pyramus' sighs. . .
'Behold the nose that mars the harmony
Of its master's phiz! blushing its treachery!'
--Such, my dear sir, is what you might have said,
Had you of wit or letters the least jot:
But, O most lamentable man!--of wit
You never had an atom, and of letters
You have three letters only!--they spell Ass!
And--had you had the necessary wit,
To serve me all the pleasantries I quote
Before this noble audience. . .e'en so,
You would not have been let to utter one--
Nay, not the half or quarter of such jest!
I take them from myself all in good part,

But not from any other man that breathes!

DE GUICHE [trying to draw away the dismayed viscount].
Come away, Viscount!

THE VISCOUNT [choking with rage].
Hear his arrogance!
A country lout who. . .who. . .has got no gloves!
Who goes out without sleeve-knots, ribbons, lace!

CYRANO.
True; all my elegances are within.
I do not prank myself out, puppy-like;
My toilet is more thorough, if less gay;
I would not sally forth--a half-washed-out
Affront upon my cheek--a conscience
Yellow-eyed, bilious, from its sodden sleep,
A ruffled honor,. . .scruples grimed and dull!
I show no bravery of shining gems.
Truth, Independence, are my fluttering plumes.
'Tis not my form I lace to make me slim,
But brace my soul with efforts as with stays,
Covered with exploits, not with ribbon-knots,
My spirit bristling high like your mustaches,
I, traversing the crowds and chattering groups
Make Truth ring bravely out like clash of spurs!

THE VISCOUNT.
But, Sir. . .

CYRANO.
I wear no gloves? And what of that?
I had one,. . .remnant of an old worn pair,
And, knowing not what else to do with it,
I threw it in the face of. . .some young fool.

THE VISCOUNT.
Base scoundrel! Rascally flat-footed lout!

CYRANO [taking off his hat, and bowing as if the viscount had intro-
duced himself].
Ah?. . .and I, Cyrano Savinien
Hercule de Bergerac

[Laughter.]

THE VISCOUNT [angrily].
Buffoon!

CYRANO [calling out as if he had been seized with the cramp].
Aie! Aie!

THE VISCOUNT [who was going away, turns back].
What on earth is the fellow saying now?

CYRANO [with grimaces of pain].
It must be moved--it's getting stiff, I vow,
--This comes of leaving it in idleness!
Aie!. . .

THE VISCOUNT.
What ails you?

CYRANO.
The cramp! cramp in my sword!

THE VISCOUNT [drawing his sword].
Good!

CYRANO.
You shall feel a charming little stroke!

THE VISCOUNT [contemptuously].
Poet!. . .

CYRANO.
Ay, poet, Sir! In proof of which,
While we fence, presto! all extempore
I will compose a ballade.

THE VISCOUNT.
A ballade?

CYRANO.
Belike you know not what a ballade is.

THE VISCOUNT.
But. . .

CYRANO [reciting, as if repeating a lesson].
Know then that the ballade should contain
Three eight-versed couplets. . .

THE VISCOUNT [stamping].
Oh!

CYRANO [still reciting].
And an envoi
Of four lines. . .

THE VISCOUNT.
You. . .

CYRANO.
I'll make one while we fight;
And touch you at the final line.

THE VISCOUNT.

No!

CYRANO.
No?
[declaiming]
The duel in Hotel of Burgundy--fought
By De Bergerac and a good-for-naught!

THE VISCOUNT.
What may that be, an if you please?

CYRANO.
The title.

THE HOUSE [in great excitement].
Give room!--Good sport!--Make place!--Fair play!--No noise!

[Tableau. A circle of curious spectators in the pit; the marquises and
officers mingled with the common people; the pages climbing on each
other's shoulders to see better. All the women standing up in the
boxes. To the right, De Guiche and his retinue. Left, Le Bret,
Ragueneau, Cyrano, etc.]

CYRANO [shutting his eyes for a second].
Wait while I choose my rhymes. . .I have them now!
[He suits the action to each word.]
I gayly doff my beaver low,
And, freeing hand and heel,
My heavy mantle off I throw,
And I draw my polished steel;
Graceful as Phoebus, round I wheel,
Alert as Scaramouch,
A word in your ear, Sir Spark, I steal--
At the envoi's end, I touch!
[They engage.]
Better for you had you lain low;

Where skewer my cock? In the heel?--
In the heart, your ribbon blue below?--
In the hip, and make you kneel?
Ho for the music of clashing steel!
--What now?--A hit? Not much!
'Twill be in the paunch the stroke I steal,
When, at the envoi, I touch.
Oh, for a rhyme, a rhyme in o?--
You wriggle, starch-white, my eel?
A rhyme! a rhyme! The white feather you SHOW!
Tac! I parry the point of your steel;
--The point you hoped to make me feel;
I open the line, now clutch
Your spit, Sir Scullion--slow your zeal!
At the envoi's end, I touch.
[He declaims solemnly.]
Envoi.
Prince, pray Heaven for your soul's weal!
I move a pace--lo, such! and such!
Cut over--feint!
[Thrusting]
What ho! You reel?
[The viscount staggers. Cyrano salutes.]
At the envoi's end, I touch!

[Acclamations. Applause in the boxes. Flowers and handkerchiefs are
     thrown down. The officers surround Cyrano, congratulating him.
Ragueneau dances for joy. Le Bret is happy, but anxious. The viscount's
     friends hold him up and bear him away.]

THE CROWD [with one long shout].
Ah!

A TROOPER.
'Tis superb!

A WOMAN.
A pretty stroke!

RAGUENEAU.
A marvel!

A MARQUIS.
A novelty!

LE BRET.
O madman!

THE CROWD [presses round Cyrano. Chorus of].
Compliments!
Bravo! Let me congratulate!. . .Quite unsurpassed!. . .

A WOMAN'S VOICE.
There is a hero for you!. . .

A MUSKETEER [advancing to Cyrano with outstretched hand].
Sir, permit;
Naught could be finer--I'm a judge I think;
I stamped, i' faith!--to show my admiration!

[He goes away.]

CYRANO [to Cuigy].
Who is that gentleman?

CUIGY.
Why--D'Artagnan!

LE BRET [to Cyrano, taking his arm].
A word with you!. . .

CYRANO.

Wait; let the rabble go!. . .
[To Bellerose]
May I stay?

BELLEROSE [respectfully].
Without doubt!

[Cries are heard outside.]

JODELET [who has looked out].
They hoot Montfleury!

BELLEROSE [solemnly].
Sic transit!. . .
[To the porters]
Sweep—close all, but leave the lights.
We sup, but later on we must return,
For a rehearsal of to-morrow's farce.

[Jodelet and Bellerose go out, bowing low to Cyrano.]

THE PORTER [to Cyrano].
You do not dine, Sir?

CYRANO.
No.

[The porter goes out.]

LE BRET.
Because?

CYRANO [proudly].
Because. . .
[Changing his tone as the porter goes away].
I have no money!. . .

LE BRET [with the action of throwing a bag].
How! The bag of crowns?...

CYRANO.
Paternal bounty, in a day, thou'rt sped!

LE BRET.
How live the next month?...

CYRANO.
I have nothing left.

LE BRET.
Folly!

CYRANO.
But what a graceful action! Think!

THE BUFFET-GIRL [coughing, behind her counter].
Hum!
[Cyrano and Le Bret turn. She comes timidly forward.]
Sir, my heart mislikes to know you fast.
[Showing the buffet]
See, all you need. Serve yourself!

CYRANO [taking off his hat].
Gentle child,
Although my Gascon pride would else forbid
To take the least bestowal from your hands,
My fear of wounding you outweighs that pride,
And bids accept...
[He goes to the buffet.]
A trifle!...These few grapes.
[She offers him the whole bunch. He takes a few.]
Nay, but this bunch!...
[She tries to give him wine, but he stops her.]

A glass of water fair!. . .
And half a macaroon!

[He gives back the other half.]

LE BRET.
What foolery!

THE BUFFET-GIRL.
Take something else!

CYRANO.
I take your hand to kiss.

[He kisses her hand as though she were a princess.]

THE BUFFET-GIRL.
Thank you, kind Sir!
[She courtesies.]
Good-night.

[She goes out.]

Act I. Scene V.

[Cyrano, Le Bret.]

CYRANO [to Le Bret].
Now talk—I listen.
[He stands at the buffet, and placing before him first the macaroon.]
Dinner!. . .
[then the grapes]
Dessert!. . .
[then the glass of water]
Wine!. . .
[he seats himself]

So! And now to table!
Ah! I was hungry, friend, nay, ravenous!
[eating]
You said--?

LE BRET.
These fops, would-be belligerent,
Will, if you heed them only, turn your head!. . .
Ask people of good sense if you would know
The effect of your fine insolence--

CYRANO [finishing his macaroon].
Enormous!

LE BRET.
The Cardinal. . .

CYRANO [radiant].
The Cardinal--was there?

LE BRET.
Must have thought it. . .

CYRANO.
Original, i' faith!

LE BRET.
But. . .

CYRANO.
He's an author. 'Twill not fail to please him
That I should mar a brother-author's play.

LE BRET.
You make too many enemies by far!

CYRANO [eating his grapes].
How many think you I have made to-night?

LE BRET.
Forty, no less, not counting ladies.

CYRANO.
Count!

LE BRET.
Montfleury first, the bourgeois, then De Guiche,
The Viscount, Baro, the Academy. . .

CYRANO.
Enough! I am o'erjoyed!

LE BRET.
But these strange ways,
Where will they lead you, at the end? Explain
Your system--come!

CYRANO.
I in a labyrinth
Was lost--too many different paths to choose;
I took. . .

LE BRET.
Which?

CYRANO.
Oh! by far the simplest path. . .
Decided to be admirable in all!

LE BRET [shrugging his shoulders].
So be it! But the motive of your hate
To Montfleury--come, tell me!

CYRANO [rising].
This Silenus,
Big-bellied, coarse, still deems himself a peril--
A danger to the love of lovely ladies,
And, while he sputters out his actor's part,
Makes sheep's eyes at their boxes--goggling frog!
I hate him since the evening he presumed
To raise his eyes to hers. . .Meseemed I saw
A slug crawl slavering o'er a flower's petals!

LE BRET [stupefied].
How now? What? Can it be. . .?

CYRANO [laughing bitterly].
That I should love?. . .
[Changing his tone, gravely]
I love.

LE BRET.
And may I know?. . .You never said. . .

CYRANO.
Come now, bethink you!. . .The fond hope to be
Beloved, e'en by some poor graceless lady,
Is, by this nose of mine for aye bereft me;
--This lengthy nose which, go where'er I will,
Pokes yet a quarter-mile ahead of me;
But I may love--and who? 'Tis Fate's decree
I love the fairest--how were't otherwise?

LE BRET.
The fairest?. . .

CYRANO.
Ay, the fairest of the world,
Most brilliant--most refined--most golden-haired!

LE BRET.
Who is this lady?

CYRANO.
She's a danger mortal,
All unsuspicious--full of charms unconscious,
Like a sweet perfumed rose--a snare of nature,
Within whose petals Cupid lurks in ambush!
He who has seen her smile has known perfection,
--Instilling into trifles grace's essence,
Divinity in every careless gesture;
Not Venus' self can mount her conch blown sea-ward,
As she can step into her chaise a porteurs,
Nor Dian fleet across the woods spring-flowered,
Light as my Lady o'er the stones of Paris!. . .

LE BRET.
Sapristi! all is clear!

CYRANO.
As spiderwebs!

LE BRET.
Your cousin, Madeleine Robin?

CYRANO.
Roxane!

LE BRET.
Well, but so much the better! Tell her so!
She saw your triumph here this very night!

CYRANO.
Look well at me--then tell me, with what hope
This vile protuberance can inspire my heart!
I do not lull me with illusions--yet

At times I'm weak: in evening hours dim
I enter some fair pleasance, perfumed sweet;
With my poor ugly devil of a nose
I scent spring's essence--in the silver rays
I see some knight--a lady on his arm,
And think 'To saunter thus 'neath the moonshine,
I were fain to have my lady, too, beside!'
Thought soars to ecstasy. . .O sudden fall!
--The shadow of my profile on the wall!

LE BRET [tenderly].
My friend!. . .

CYRANO.
My friend, at times 'tis hard, 'tis bitter,
To feel my loneliness--my own ill-favor. . .

LE BRET [taking his hand].
You weep?

CYRANO.
No, never! Think, how vilely suited
Adown this nose a tear its passage tracing!
I never will, while of myself I'm master,
let the divinity of tears--their beauty
Be wedded to such common ugly grossness.
Nothing more solemn than a tear--sublimer;
And I would not by weeping turn to laughter
The grave emotion that a tear engenders!

LE BRET.
Never be sad! What's love?--a chance of Fortune!

CYRANO [shaking his head].
Look I a Caesar to woo Cleopatra?
A Tito to aspire to Berenice?

LE BRET.
Your courage and your wit!--The little maid
Who offered you refreshment even now,
Her eyes did not abhor you--you saw well!

CYRANO [impressed].
True!

LE BRET.
Well, how then?. . .I saw Roxane herself
Was death-pale as she watched the duel.

CYRANO.
Pale?

LE BRET.
Her heart, her fancy, are already caught!
Put it to th' touch!

CYRANO.
That she may mock my face?
That is the one thing on this earth I fear!

THE PORTER [introducing some one to Cyrano].
Sir, some one asks for you. . .

CYRANO [seeing the duenna].
God! her duenna!

Act I. Scene VI.

[Cyrano, Le Bret, the duenna.]

THE DUENNA [with a low bow].
I was bid ask you where a certain lady
Could see her valiant cousin--but in secret.

CYRANO [overwhelmed].
See me?

THE DUENNA [courtesying].
Ay, Sir! She has somewhat to tell.

CYRANO.
Somewhat?. . .

THE DUENNA [still courtesying].
Ay, private matters!

CYRANO [staggering].
Ah, my God!

THE DUENNA.
To-morrow, at the early blush of dawn,
We go to hear mass at St. Roch.

CYRANO [leaning against Le Bret].
My God!

THE DUENNA.
After--what place for a few minutes' speech?

CYRANO [confused].
Where? Ah!. . .but. . .Ah, my God!. . .

THE DUENNA.
Say!

CYRANO.
I reflect!. . .

THE DUENNA.
Where?

CYRANO.
At--the pastry-house of Ragueneau.

THE DUENNA.
Where lodges he?

CYRANO.
The Rue--God!--St. Honore!

THE DUENNA [going].
Good. Be you there. At seven.

CYRANO.
Without fail.

[The duenna goes out.]

Act I. Scene VII.

[Cyrano, Le Bret. Then actors, actresses, Cuigy, Brissaille, Ligniere, the porter, the violinists.]

CYRANO [falling into Le Bret's arms].
A rendezvous. . .from her!. . .

LE BRET.
You're sad no more!

CYRANO.
Ah! Let the world go burn! She knows I live!

LE BRET.
Now you'll be calm, I hope?

CYRANO [beside himself for joy].
Calm? I now calm?

I'll be frenetic, frantic,--raving mad!
Oh, for an army to attack!--a host!
I've ten hearts in my breast; a score of arms;
No dwarfs to cleave in twain!. . .
[Wildly]
No! Giants now!

[For a few moments the shadows of the actors have been moving on
the stage, whispers are heard--the rehearsal is beginning. The violinists
are in their places.]

A VOICE FROM THE STAGE.
Hollo there! Silence! We rehearse!

CYRANO [laughing].
We go!

[He moves away. By the big door enter Cuigy, Brissaille, and some
officers, holding up Ligniere, who is drunk.]

CUIGY.
Cyrano!

CYRANO.
Well, what now?

CUIGY.
A lusty thrush
They're bringing you!

CYRANO [recognizing him].
Ligniere!. . .What has chanced?

CUIGY.
He seeks you!

BRISSAILLE.
He dare not go home!

CYRANO.
Why not?

LIGNIERE [in a husky voice, showing him a crumpled letter].
This letter warns me. . .that a hundred men. . .
Revenge that threatens me. . .that song, you know--
At the Porte de Nesle. To get to my own house
I must pass there. . .I dare not!. . .Give me leave
To sleep to-night beneath your roof! Allow. . .

CYRANO.
A hundred men? You'll sleep in your own bed!

LIGNIERE [frightened].
But--

CYRANO [in a terrible voice, showing him the lighted lantern held by
the porter, who is listening curiously].
Take the lantern.
[Ligniere seizes it.]
Let us start! I swear
That I will make your bed to-night myself!
[To the officers]
Follow; some stay behind, as witnesses!

CUIGY.
A hundred!. . .

CYRANO.
Less, to-night--would be too few!

[The actors and actresses, in their costumes, have come down from the
stage, and are listening.]

LE BRET.
But why embroil yourself?

CYRANO.
Le Bret who scolds!

LE BRET.
That worthless drunkard!--

CYRANO [slapping Ligniere on the shoulder].
Wherefore? For this cause;--
This wine-barrel, this cask of Burgundy,
Did, on a day, an action full of grace;
As he was leaving church, he saw his love
Take holy water--he, who is affeared
At water's taste, ran quickly to the stoup,
And drank it all, to the last drop!. . .

AN ACTRESS.
Indeed, that was a graceful thing!

CYRANO.
Ay, was it not?

THE ACTRESS [to the others].
But why a hundred men 'gainst one poor rhymer?

CYRANO.
March!
[To the officers]
Gentlemen, when you shall see me charge,
Bear me no succor, none, whate'er the odds!

ANOTHER ACTRESS [jumping from the stage].
Oh! I shall come and see!

CYRANO.
Come, then!

ANOTHER [jumping down--to an old actor].
And you?. . .

CYRANO.
Come all--the Doctor, Isabel, Leander,
Come, for you shall add, in a motley swarm,
The farce Italian to this Spanish drama!

ALL THE WOMEN [dancing for joy].
Bravo!--a mantle, quick!--my hood!

JODELET.
Come on!

CYRANO.
Play us a march, gentlemen of the band!
[The violinists join the procession, which is forming. They take the
footlights, and divide them for torches.]
Brave officers! next, women in costume,
And, twenty paces on--
[He takes his place.]
I all alone,
Beneath the plume that Glory lends, herself,
To deck my beaver--proud as Scipio!. . .
--You hear me?--I forbid you succor me!--
One, two three! Porter, open wide the doors!
[The porter opens the doors; a view of old Paris in the moonlight
is seen.]
Ah!. . .Paris wrapped in night! half nebulous:
The moonlight streams o'er the blue-shadowed roofs;
A lovely frame for this wild battle-scene;
Beneath the vapor's floating scarves, the Seine
Trembles, mysterious, like a magic mirror,

And, shortly, you shall see what you shall see!

ALL.
To the Porte de Nesle!

CYRANO [standing on the threshold].
Ay, to the Porte de Nesle!
[Turning to the actress]
Did you not ask, young lady, for what cause
Against this rhymer fivescore men were sent?
[He draws his sword; then, calmly]
'Twas that they knew him for a friend of mine!

[He goes out. Ligniere staggers first after him, then the actresses on the officers' arms--the actors. The procession starts to the sound of the violins and in the faint light of the candles.]

[Curtain.]

ACT II

The Poet's Eating-House.

Ragueneau's cook and pastry-shop. A large kitchen at the corner of the Rue St. Honore and the Rue de l'Arbre Sec, which are seen in the background through the glass door, in the gray dawn.

On the left, in the foreground, a counter, surmounted by a stand in forged iron, on which are hung geese, ducks, and water peacocks. In great china vases are tall bouquets of simple flowers, principally yellow sunflowers.

On the same side, farther back, an immense open fireplace, in front of which, between monster firedogs, on each of which hangs a little saucepan; the roasts are dripping into the pans.

On the right, foreground with door.

Farther back, staircase leading to a little room under the roof, the entrance of which is visible through the open shutter. In this room a table is laid. A small Flemish luster is alight. It is a place for eating and drinking. A wooden gallery, continuing the staircase, apparently leads to other similar little rooms.

In the middle of the shop an iron hoop is suspended from the ceiling by a string with which it can be drawn up and down, and big game is hung around it.

The ovens in the darkness under the stairs give forth a red glow. The copper pans shine. The spits are turning. Heaps of food formed into pyramids. Hams suspended. It is the busy hour of the morning. Bustle and hurry of scullions, fat cooks, and diminutive apprentices, their caps profusely decorated with cock's feathers and wings of guinea-fowl.

On metal and wicker plates they are bringing in piles of cakes and tarts.

Tables laden with rolls and dishes of food. Other tables surrounded with chairs are ready for the consumers.

A small table in a corner covered with papers, at which Ragueneau is seated writing on the rising of the curtain.

Act II. Scene I.

[Ragueneau, pastry-cooks, then Lise. Ragueneau is writing, with an inspired air, at a small table, and counting on his fingers.]

FIRST PASTRY-COOK [bringing in an elaborate fancy dish].
Fruits in nougat!

SECOND PASTRY-COOK [bringing another dish].
Custard!

THIRD PASTRY-COOK [bringing a roast, decorated with feathers].
Peacock!

FOURTH PASTRY-COOK [bringing a batch of cakes on a slab].
Rissoles!

FIFTH PASTRY-COOK [bringing a sort of pie-dish].
Beef jelly!

RAGUENEAU [ceasing to write, and raising his head].
Aurora's silver rays begin to glint e'en now on the copper pans, and
thou, O Ragueneau! must perforce stifle in thy breast the God of Song!
Anon shall come the hour of the lute!--now 'tis the hour of the oven!
[He rises. To a cook]
You, make that sauce longer, 'tis too short!

THE COOK.
How much too short?

RAGUENEAU.
Three feet.

[He passes on farther.]

THE COOK.
What means he?

FIRST PASTRY-COOK [showing a dish to Ragueneau].
The tart!

SECOND PASTRY-COOK.
The pie!

RAGUENEAU [before the fire].
My muse, retire, lest thy bright eyes be reddened by the fagot's blaze!
[To a cook, showing him some loaves]
You have put the cleft o' th' loaves in the wrong place; know you not
that the coesura should be between the hemistiches?
[To another, showing him an unfinished pasty]

To this palace of paste you must add the roof. . .
[To a young apprentice, who, seated on the ground, is spitting
the fowls]
And you, as you put on your lengthy spit the modest fowl and the
superb turkey, my son, alternate them, as the old Malherbe loved well
to alternate his long lines of verse with the short ones; thus shall your
roasts, in strophes, turn before the flame!

ANOTHER APPRENTICE [also coming up with a tray covered by a
napkin].
Master, I bethought me erewhile of your tastes, and made this, which
will please you, I hope.

[He uncovers the tray, and shows a large lyre made of pastry.]

RAGUENEAU [enchanted].
A lyre!

THE APPRENTICE.
'Tis of brioche pastry.

RAGUENEAU [touched].
With conserved fruits.

THE APPRENTICE.
The strings, see, are of sugar.

RAGUENEAU [giving him a coin].
Go, drink my health!
[Seeing Lise enter]
Hush! My wife. Bustle, pass on, and hide that money!
[To Lise, showing her the lyre, with a conscious look]
Is it not beautiful?

LISE.
'Tis passing silly!

[She puts a pile of papers on the counter.]

RAGUENEAU.
Bags? Good. I thank you.
[He looks at them.]
Heavens! my cherished leaves! The poems of my friends! Torn, dismembered,
to make bags for holding biscuits and cakes!. . .Ah, 'tis the old tale again.
. .Orpheus and the Bacchantes!

LISE [dryly].
And am I not free to turn at last to some use the sole thing that your wretched scribblers of halting lines leave behind them by way of payment?

RAGUENEAU.
Groveling ant!. . .Insult not the divine grasshoppers, the sweet singers!

LISE.
Before you were the sworn comrade of all that crew, my friend, you did not call your wife ant and Bacchante!

RAGUENEAU.
To turn fair verse to such a use!

LISE.
'Faith, 'tis all it's good for.

RAGUENEAU.
Pray then, madam, to what use would you degrade prose?

Act II. Scene II.

[The same. Two children, who have just trotted into the shop.]

RAGUENEAU.
What would you, little ones?

FIRST CHILD.
Three pies.

RAGUENEAU [serving them].
See, hot and well browned.

SECOND CHILD.
If it please you, Sir, will you wrap them up for us?

RAGUENEAU [aside, distressed].
Alas! one of my bags!
[To the children]
What? Must I wrap them up?
[He takes a bag, and just as he is about to put in the pies, he reads]
'Ulysses thus, on leaving fair Penelope. . .'
Not that one!
[He puts it aside, and takes another, and as he is about to put in the pies, he reads]
'The gold-locked Phoebus. . .'
Nay, nor that one!. . .

[Same play.]

LISE [impatiently].
What are you dallying for?

RAGUENEAU.
Here! here! here
[He chooses a third, resignedly.]
The sonnet to Phillis!. . .but 'tis hard to part with it!

LISE.
By good luck he has made up his mind at last!

[Shrugging her shoulders]
Nicodemus!

[She mounts on a chair, and begins to range plates on a dresser.]

RAGUENEAU [taking advantage of the moment she turns her back,
calls back the children, who are already at the door].
Hist! children!. . .render me back the sonnet to Phillis, and you shall
have six pies instead of three.

[The children give him back the bag, seize the cakes quickly, and
go out.]

RAGUENEAU [smoothing out the paper, begins to declaim].
'Phillis!. . .' On that sweet name a smear of butter! 'Phillis!. . .'

[Cyrano enters hurriedly.]

Act II. Scene III.

[Ragueneau, Lise, Cyrano, then the musketeer.]

CYRANO.
What's o'clock?

RAGUENEAU [bowing low].
Six o'clock.

CYRANO [with emotion].
In one hour's time!

[He paces up and down the shop.]

RAGUENEAU [following him].
Bravo! I saw. . .

CYRANO.
Well, what saw you, then?

RAGUENEAU.
Your combat!. . .

CYRANO.
Which?

RAGUENEAU.
That in the Burgundy Hotel, 'faith!

CYRANO [contemptuously].
Ah!. . .the duel!

RAGUENEAU [admiringly].
Ay! the duel in verse!. . .

LISE.
He can talk of naught else!

CYRANO.
Well! Good! let be!

RAGUENEAU [making passes with a spit that he catches up].
'At the envoi's end, I touch!. . .At the envoi's end, I touch!'. . .'Tis
fine, fine!
[With increasing enthusiasm]
'At the envoi's end--'

CYRANO.
What hour is it now, Ragueneau?

RAGUENEAU [stopping short in the act of thrusting to look at
the clock].
Five minutes after six!. . .'I touch!'

[He straightens himself.]
. . .Oh! to write a ballade!

LISE [to Cyrano, who, as he passes by the counter, has absently shaken hands with her].
What's wrong with your hand?

CYRANO.
Naught; a slight cut.

RAGUENEAU.
Have you been in some danger?

CYRANO.
None in the world.

LISE [shaking her finger at him].
Methinks you speak not the truth in saying that!

CYRANO.
Did you see my nose quiver when I spoke? 'Faith, it must have been a monstrous lie that should move it!
[Changing his tone]
I wait some one here. Leave us alone, and disturb us for naught an it were not for crack of doom!

RAGUENEAU.
But 'tis impossible; my poets are coming. . .

LISE [ironically].
Oh, ay, for their first meal o' the day!

CYRANO.
Prythee, take them aside when I shall make you sign to do so. . .What's o'clock?

RAGUENEAU.
Ten minutes after six.

CYRANO [nervously seating himself at Ragueneau's table, and drawing some paper toward him].
A pen!. . .

RAGUENEAU [giving him the one from behind his ear].
Here--a swan's quill.

A MUSKETEER [with fierce mustache, enters, and in a stentorian voice].
Good-day!

[Lise goes up to him quickly.]

CYRANO [turning round].
Who's that?

RAGUENEAU.
'Tis a friend of my wife--a terrible warrior--at least so says he himself.

CYRANO [taking up the pen, and motioning Ragueneau away].
Hush!
[To himself]
I will write, fold it, give it her, and fly!
[Throws down the pen]
Coward!. . .But strike me dead if I dare to speak to her,. . .ay, even one single word!
[To Ragueneau]
What time is it?

RAGUENEAU.
A quarter after six!. . .

CYRANO [striking his breast].

Ay--a single word of all those here! here! But writing, 'tis easier done. . .
[He takes up the pen.]
Go to, I will write it, that love-letter! Oh! I have writ it and rewrit it
in my own mind so oft that it lies there ready for pen and ink; and if
I lay
but my soul by my letter-sheet, 'tis naught to do but to copy from it.

[He writes. Through the glass of the door the silhouettes of their
figures move uncertainly and hesitatingly.]

Act II. Scene IV.

[Ragueneau, Lise, the musketeer. Cyrano at the little table writing.
The poets, dressed in black, their stockings ungartered, and covered
with mud.]

LISE [entering, to Ragueneau].
Here they come, your mud-bespattered friends!

FIRST POET [entering, to Ragueneau].
Brother in art!. . .

SECOND POET [to Ragueneau, shaking his hands].
Dear brother!

THIRD POET.
High soaring eagle among pastry-cooks!
[He sniffs.]
Marry! it smells good here in your eyrie!

FOURTH POET.
'Tis at Phoebus' own rays that thy roasts turn!

FIFTH POET.
Apollo among master-cooks--

RAGUENEAU [whom they surround and embrace].
Ah! how quick a man feels at his ease with them!. . .

FIRST POET.
We were stayed by the mob; they are crowded all round the Porte
de Nesle!. . .

SECOND POET.
Eight bleeding brigand carcasses strew the pavements there--all slit
open with sword-gashes!

CYRANO [raising his head a minute].
Eight?. . .hold, methought seven.

[He goes on writing.]

RAGUENEAU [to Cyrano].
Know you who might be the hero of the fray?

CYRANO [carelessly].
Not I.

LISE [to the musketeer].
And you? Know you?

THE MUSKETEER [twirling his mustache].
Maybe!

CYRANO [writing a little way off:--he is heard murmuring a word
from time to time].
'I love thee!'

FIRST POET.
'Twas one man, say they all, ay, swear to it, one man who, single-
handed, put the whole band to the rout!

SECOND POET.
'Twas a strange sight!--pikes and cudgels strewed thick upon the ground.

CYRANO [writing].
. . .'Thine eyes'. . .

THIRD POET.
And they were picking up hats all the way to the Quai d'Orfevres!

FIRST POET.
Sapristi! but he must have been a ferocious. . .

CYRANO [same play].
. . .'Thy lips'. . .

FIRST POET.
'Twas a parlous fearsome giant that was the author of such exploits!

CYRANO [same play].
. . .'And when I see thee come, I faint for fear.'

SECOND POET [filching a cake].
What hast rhymed of late, Ragueneau?

CYRANO [same play].
. . .'Who worships thee'. . .
[He stops, just as he is about to sign, and gets up, slipping the letter into his doublet.]
No need I sign, since I give it her myself.

RAGUENEAU [to second poet].
I have put a recipe into verse.

THIRD POET [seating himself by a plate of cream-puffs].
Go to! Let us hear these verses!

FOURTH POET [looking at a cake which he has taken].
Its cap is all a' one side!

[He makes one bite of the top.]

FIRST POET.
See how this gingerbread woos the famished rhymer with its almond
eyes, and its eyebrows of angelica!

[He takes it.]

SECOND POET.
We listen.

THIRD POET [squeezing a cream-puff gently].
How it laughs! Till its very cream runs over!

SECOND POET [biting a bit off the great lyre of pastry].
This is the first time in my life that ever I drew any means of nourishing me from the lyre!

RAGUENEAU [who has put himself ready for reciting, cleared his
throat, settled his cap, struck an attitude].
A recipe in verse!. . .

SECOND POET [to first, nudging him].
You are breakfasting?

FIRST POET [to second].
And you dining, methinks.

RAGUENEAU.
How almond tartlets are made.
Beat your eggs up, light and quick;
Froth them thick;
Mingle with them while you beat

Juice of lemon, essence fine;
Then combine
The burst milk of almonds sweet.
Circle with a custard paste
The slim waist
Of your tartlet-molds; the top
With a skillful finger print,
Nick and dint,
Round their edge, then, drop by drop,
In its little dainty bed
Your cream shed:
In the oven place each mold:
Reappearing, softly browned,
The renowned
Almond tartlets you behold!

THE POETS [with mouths crammed full].
Exquisite! Delicious!

A POET [choking].
Homph!

[They go up, eating.]

CYRANO [who has been watching, goes toward Ragueneau].
Lulled by your voice, did you see how they were stuffing
themselves?

RAGUENEAU [in a low voice, smiling].
Oh, ay! I see well enough, but I never will seem to look, fearing to
distress them; thus I gain a double pleasure when I recite to them my
poems; for I leave those poor fellows who have not breakfasted free to
eat, even while I gratify my own dearest foible, see you?

CYRANO [clapping him on the shoulder].
Friend, I like you right well!. . .

[Ragueneau goes after his friends. Cyrano follows him with his eyes, then, rather sharply]
Ho there! Lise!
[Lise, who is talking tenderly to the musketeer, starts, and comes down toward Cyrano.]
So this fine captain is laying siege to you?

LISE [offended].
One haughty glance of my eye can conquer any man that should dare venture aught 'gainst my virtue.

CYRANO.
Pooh! Conquering eyes, methinks, are oft conquered eyes.

LISE [choking with anger].
But--

CYRANO [incisively].
I like Ragueneau well, and so--mark me, Dame Lise--I permit not that he be rendered a laughing-stock by any. . .

LISE.
But. . .

CYRANO [who has raised his voice so as to be heard by the gallant].
A word to the wise. . .

[He bows to the musketeer, and goes to the doorway to watch, after looking at the clock.]

LISE [to the musketeer, who has merely bowed in answer to Cyrano's bow].
How now? Is this your courage?. . .Why turn you not a jest on his nose?

THE MUSKETEER.

On his nose?. . .ay, ay. . .his nose.

[He goes quickly farther away; Lise follows him.]

CYRANO [from the doorway, signing to Ragueneau to draw the
poets away].
Hist!. . .

RAGUENEAU [showing them the door on the right].
We shall be more private there. . .

CYRANO [impatiently].
Hist! Hist!. . .

RAGUENEAU [drawing them farther].
To read poetry, 'tis better here. . .

FIRST POET [despairingly, with his mouth full].
What! leave the cakes?. . .

SECOND POET.
Never! Let's take them with us!

[They all follow Ragueneau in procession, after sweeping all the cakes
off the trays.]

Act II. Scene V.

[Cyrano, Roxane, the duenna.]

CYRANO.
Ah! if I see but the faint glimmer of hope, then I draw out my letter!
[Roxane, masked, followed by the duenna, appears at the glass pane of
the door. He opens quickly.]
Enter!. . .
[Walking up to the duenna]

Two words with you, Duenna.

THE DUENNA.
Four, Sir, an it like you.

CYRANO.
Are you fond of sweet things?

THE DUENNA.
Ay, I could eat myself sick on them!

CYRANO [catching up some of the paper bags from the counter].
Good. See you these two sonnets of Monsieur Beuserade. . .

THE DUENNA.
Hey?

CYRANO.
. . .Which I fill for you with cream cakes!

THE DUENNA [changing her expression].
Ha.

CYRANO.
What say you to the cake they call a little puff?

THE DUENNA.
If made with cream, Sir, I love them passing well.

CYRANO.
Here I plunge six for your eating into the bosom of a poem by Saint
Amant! And in these verses of Chapelain I glide a lighter morsel. Stay,
love you hot cakes?

THE DUENNA.
Ay, to the core of my heart!

CYRANO [filling her arms with the bags].
Pleasure me then; go eat them all in the street.

THE DUENNA.
But. . .

CYRANO [pushing her out].
And come not back till the very last crumb be eaten!

[He shuts the door, comes down toward Roxane, and, uncovering,
stands at a respectful distance from her.]

Act II. Scene VI.

[Cyrano, Roxane.]

CYRANO.
Blessed be the moment when you condescend--
Remembering that humbly I exist--
To come to meet me, and to say. . .to tell?. . .

ROXANE [who has unmasked].
To thank you first of all. That dandy count,
Whom you checkmated in brave sword-play
Last night,. . .he is the man whom a great lord,
Desirous of my favor. . .

CYRANO.
Ha, De Guiche?

ROXANE [casting down her eyes].
Sought to impose on me. . .for husband. . .

CYRANO.
Ay! Husband!--dupe-husband!. . .Husband a la mode!
[Bowing]

Then I fought, happy chance! sweet lady, not
For my ill favor--but your favors fair!

ROXANE.
Confession next!. . .But, ere I make my shrift,
You must be once again that brother-friend
With whom I used to play by the lake-side!. . .

CYRANO.
Ay, you would come each spring to Bergerac!

ROXANE.
Mind you the reeds you cut to make your swords?. . .

CYRANO.
While you wove corn-straw plaits for your dolls' hair!

ROXANE.
Those were the days of games!. . .

CYRANO.
And blackberries!. . .

ROXANE.
In those days you did everything I bid!. . .

CYRANO.
Roxane, in her short frock, was Madeleine. . .

ROXANE.
Was I fair then?

CYRANO.
You were not ill to see!

ROXANE.

Ofttimes, with hands all bloody from a fall,
You'd run to me! Then--aping mother-ways--
I, in a voice would-be severe, would chide,--
[She takes his hand.]
'What is this scratch, again, that I see here?'
[She starts, surprised.]
Oh! 'Tis too much! What's this?
[Cyrano tries to draw away his hand.]
No, let me see!
At your age, fie! Where did you get that scratch?

CYRANO.
I got it--playing at the Porte de Nesle.

ROXANE [seating herself by the table, and dipping her handkerchief
in a glass of water].
Give here!

CYRANO [sitting by her].
So soft! so gay maternal-sweet!

ROXANE.
And tell me, while I wipe away the blood,
How many 'gainst you?

CYRANO.
Oh! A hundred--near.

ROXANE.
Come, tell me!

CYRANO.
No, let be. But you, come tell
The thing, just now, you dared not. . .

ROXANE [keeping his hand].

Now, I dare!
The scent of those old days emboldens me!
Yes, now I dare. Listen. I am in love.

CYRANO.
Ah!. . .

ROXANE.
But with one who knows not.

CYRANO.
Ah!. . .

ROXANE.
Not yet.

CYRANO.
Ah!. . .

ROXANE.
But who, if he knows not, soon shall learn.

CYRANO.
Ah!. . .

ROXANE.
A poor youth who all this time has loved
Timidly, from afar, and dares not speak. . .

CYRANO.
Ah!. . .

ROXANE.
Leave your hand; why, it is fever-hot!--
But I have seen love trembling on his lips.

CYRANO.
Ah!. . .

ROXANE [bandaging his hand with her handkerchief].
And to think of it! that he by chance--
Yes, cousin, he is of your regiment!

CYRANO.
Ah!. . .

ROXANE [laughing].
--Is cadet in your own company!

CYRANO.
Ah!. . .

ROXANE.
On his brow he bears the genius-stamp;
He is proud, noble, young, intrepid, fair. . .

CYRANO [rising suddenly, very pale].
Fair!

ROXANE.
Why, what ails you?

CYRANO.
Nothing; 'tis. . .
[He shows his hand, smiling.]
This scratch!

ROXANE.
I love him; all is said. But you must know
I have only seen him at the Comedy. . .

CYRANO.

How? You have never spoken?

ROXANE.
Eyes can speak.

CYRANO.
How know you then that he. . .?

ROXANE.
Oh! people talk
'Neath the limes in the Place Royale. . .
Gossip's chat
Has let me know. . .

CYRANO.
He is cadet?

ROXANE.
In the Guards.

CYRANO.
His name?

ROXANE.
Baron Christian de Neuvillette.

CYRANO.
How now?. . .He is not of the Guards!

ROXANE.
To-day
He is not join your ranks, under Captain
Carbon de Castel-Jaloux.

CYRANO.
Ah, how quick,

How quick the heart has flown!...But, my poor child...

THE DUENNA [opening the door].
The cakes are eaten, Monsieur Bergerac!

CYRANO.
Then read the verses printed on the bags!
[She goes out.]
...My poor child, you who love but flowing words,
Bright wit,--what if he be a lout unskilled?

ROXANE.
No, his bright locks, like D'Urfe's heroes...

CYRANO.
Ah!
A well-curled pate, and witless tongue, perchance!

ROXANE.
Ah no! I guess--I feel--his words are fair!

CYRANO.
All words are fair that lurk 'neath fair mustache!
--Suppose he were a fool!...

ROXANE [stamping her foot].
Then bury me!

CYRANO [after a pause].
Was it to tell me this you brought me here?
I fail to see what use this serves, Madame.

ROXANE.
Nay, but I felt a terror, here, in the heart,
On learning yesterday you were Gascons
All of your company...

CYRANO.
And we provoke
All beardless sprigs that favor dares admit
'Midst us pure Gascons--(pure! Heaven save the mark!
They told you that as well?

ROXANE.
Ah! Think how I
Trembled for him!

CYRANO [between his teeth].
Not causelessly!

ROXANE.
But when
Last night I saw you,--brave, invincible,--
Punish that dandy, fearless hold your own
Against those brutes, I thought--I thought, if he
Whom all fear, all--if he would only. . .

CYRANO.
Good.
I will befriend your little Baron.

ROXANE.
Ah!
You'll promise me you will do this for me?
I've always held you as a tender friend.

CYRANO.
Ay, ay.

ROXANE.
Then you will be his friend?

CYRANO.

I swear!

ROXANE.
And he shall fight no duels, promise!

CYRANO.
None.

ROXANE.
You are kind, cousin! Now I must be gone.
[She puts on her mask and veil quickly; then, absently]
You have not told me of your last night's fray.
Ah, but it must have been a hero-fight!. . .
--Bid him to write.
[She sends him a kiss with her fingers.]
How good you are!

CYRANO.
Ay! Ay!

ROXANE.
A hundred men against you? Now, farewell.--
We are great friends?

CYRANO.
Ay, ay!

ROXANE.
Oh, bid him write!
You'll tell me all one day--A hundred men!--
Ah, brave!. . .How brave!

CYRANO [bowing to her].
I have fought better since.

   [She goes out. Cyrano stands motionless, with eyes on the ground. A silence. The door (right) opens. Ragueneau looks in.]

Act II. Scene VII.

[Cyrano, Ragueneau, poets, Carbon de Castel-Jaloux, the cadets, a crowd, then De Guiche.]

RAGUENEAU.
Can we come in?

CYRANO [without stirring].
Yes. . .

[Ragueneau signs to his friends, and they come in. At the same time, by door at back, enters Carbon de Castel-Jaloux, in Captain's uniform. He makes gestures of surprise on seeing Cyrano.]

CARBON.
Here he is!

CYRANO [raising his head].
Captain!. . .

CARBON [delightedly].
Our hero! We heard all! Thirty or more
Of my cadets are there!. . .

CYRANO [shrinking back].
But. . .

CARBON [trying to draw him away].
Come with me!
They will not rest until they see you!

CYRANO.
No!

CARBON.
They're drinking opposite, at The Bear's Head.

CYRANO.
I...

CARBON [going to the door and calling across the street in a voice of thunder].
He won't come! The hero's in the sulks!

A VOICE [outside].
Ah! Sandious!

[Tumult outside. Noise of boots and swords is heard approaching.]

CARBON [rubbing his hands].
They are running 'cross the street!

CADETS [entering].
Mille dious! Capdedious! Pocapdedious!

RAGUENEAU [drawing back startled].
Gentlemen, are you all from Gascony?

THE CADETS.
All!

A CADET [to Cyrano].
Bravo!

CYRANO.
Baron!

ANOTHER [shaking his hands].
Vivat!

CYRANO.
Baron!

THIRD CADET.
Come!
I must embrace you!

CYRANO.
Baron!

SEVERAL GASCONS.
We'll embrace
Him, all in turn!

CYRANO [not knowing whom to reply to].
Baron!. . .Baron!. . .I beg. . .

RAGUENEAU.
Are you all Barons, Sirs?

THE CADETS.
Ay, every one!

RAGUENEAU.
Is it true?. . .

FIRST CADET.
Ay--why, you could build a tower
With nothing but our coronets, my friend!

LE BRET [entering, and running up to Cyrano].
They're looking for you! Here's a crazy mob
Led by the men who followed you last night. . .

CYRANO [alarmed].
What! Have you told them where to find me?

LE BRET [rubbing his hands].
Yes!

A BURGHER [entering, followed by a group of men].
Sir, all the Marais is a-coming here!

[Outside the street has filled with people. Chaises a porteurs and
carriages have drawn up.]

LE BRET [in a low voice, smiling, to Cyrano]
And Roxane?

CYRANO [quickly].
Hush!

THE CROWD [calling outside].
Cyrano!. . .

[A crowd rush into the shop, pushing one another. Acclamations.]

RAGUENEAU [standing on a table].
Lo! my shop
Invaded! They break all! Magnificent!

PEOPLE [crowding round Cyrano].
My friend!. . .my friend. . .

CYRANO.
Meseems that yesterday
I had not all these friends!

LE BRET [delighted].
Success!

A YOUNG MARQUIS [hurrying up with his hands held out].
My friend,

Didst thou but know. . .

CYRANO.
Thou!. . .Marry!. . .thou!. . .Pray when
Did we herd swine together, you and I!

ANOTHER.
I would present you, Sir, to some fair dames
Who in my carriage yonder. . .

CYRANO [coldly].
Ah! and who
Will first present you, Sir, to me?

LE BRET [astonished].
What's wrong?

CYRANO.
Hush!

A MAN OF LETTERS [with writing-board].
A few details?. . .

CYRANO.
No.

LE BRET [nudging his elbow].
'Tis Theophrast,
Renaudet,. . .of the 'Court Gazette'!

CYRANO.
Who cares?

LE BRET.
This paper--but it is of great importance!. . .
They say it will be an immense success!

A POET [advancing].
Sir. . .

CYRANO.
What, another!

THE POET.
. . .Pray permit I make
A pentacrostic on your name. . .

SOME ONE [also advancing].
Pray, Sir. . .

CYRANO.
Enough! Enough!

[A movement in the crowd. De Guiche appears, escorted by officers.
Cuigy, Brissaille, the officers who went with Cyrano the night before.
Cuigy comes rapidly up to Cyrano.]

CUIGY [to Cyrano].
Here is Monsieur de Guiche?
[A murmur--every one makes way].
He comes from the Marshal of Gassion!

DE GUICHE [bowing to Cyrano].
. . .Who would express his admiration, Sir,
For your new exploit noised so loud abroad.

THE CROWD.
Bravo!

CYRANO [bowing].
The Marshal is a judge of valor.

DE GUICHE.

He could not have believed the thing, unless
These gentlemen had sworn they witnessed it.

CUIGY.
With our own eyes!

LE BRET [aside to Cyrano, who has an absent air].
But. . .you. . .

CYRANO.
Hush!

LE BRET.
But. . .You suffer?

CYRANO [starting].
Before this rabble?--I?. . .
[He draws himself up, twirls his mustache, and throws back his
shoulders.]
Wait!. . .You shall see!

DE GUICHE [to whom Cuigy has spoken in a low voice].
In feats of arms, already your career
Abounded.--You serve with those crazy pates
Of Gascons?

CYRANO.
Ay, with the Cadets.

A CADET [in a terrible voice].
With us!

DE GUICHE [looking at the cadets, ranged behind Cyrano].
Ah!. . .All these gentlemen of haughty mien,
Are they the famous?. . .

CARBON.
Cyrano!

CYRANO.
Ay, Captain!

CARBON.
Since all my company's assembled here,
Pray favor me,--present them to my lord!

CYRANO [making two steps toward De Guiche].
My Lord de Guiche, permit that I present--
[pointing to the cadets]
The bold Cadets of Gascony,
Of Carbon of Castel-Jaloux!
Brawling and swaggering boastfully,
The bold Cadets of Gascony!
Spouting of Armory, Heraldry,
Their veins a-brimming with blood so blue,
The bold Cadets of Gascony,
Of Carbon of Castel-Jaloux:
Eagle-eye, and spindle-shanks,
Fierce mustache, and wolfish tooth!
Slash-the-rabble and scatter-their-ranks;
Eagle-eye and spindle-shanks,
With a flaming feather that gayly pranks,
Hiding the holes in their hats, forsooth!
Eagle-eye and spindle-shanks,
Fierce mustache, and wolfish tooth!
'Pink-your-Doublet' and 'Slit-your-Trunk'
Are their gentlest sobriquets;
With Fame and Glory their soul is drunk!
'Pink-your-Doublet' and 'Slit-your-Trunk,'
In brawl and skirmish they show their spunk,
Give rendezvous in broil and fray;
'Pink-your-Doublet' and 'Slit-your-Trunk'

Are their gentlest sobriquets!
What, ho! Cadets of Gascony!
All jealous lovers are sport for you!
O Woman! dear divinity!
What, ho! Cadets of Gascony!
Whom scowling husbands quake to see.
Blow, 'taratara,' and cry 'Cuckoo.'
What, ho! Cadets of Gascony!
Husbands and lovers are game for you!

DE GUICHE [seated with haughty carelessness in an armchair
brought quickly by Ragueneau].
A poet! 'Tis the fashion of the hour!
--Will you be mine?

CYRANO.
No, Sir,--no man's!

DE GUICHE.
Last night
Your fancy pleased my uncle Richelieu.
I'll gladly say a word to him for you.

LE BRET [overjoyed].
Great Heavens!

DE GUICHE.
I imagine you have rhymed
Five acts, or so?

LE BRET [in Cyrano's ear].
Your play!--your 'Agrippine!'
You'll see it staged at last!

DE GUICHE.
Take them to him.

CYRANO [beginning to be tempted and attracted].
In sooth,--I would. . .

DE GUICHE.
He is a critic skilled:
He may correct a line or two, at most.

CYRANO [whose face stiffens at once].
Impossible! My blood congeals to think
That other hand should change a comma's dot.

DE GUICHE.
But when a verse approves itself to him
He pays it dear, good friend.

CYRANO.
He pays less dear
Than I myself; when a verse pleases me
I pay myself, and sing it to myself!

DE GUICHE.
You are proud.

CYRANO.
Really? You have noticed that?

A CADET [entering, with a string of old battered plumed beaver hats,
full of holes, slung on his sword].
See, Cyrano,--this morning, on the quay
What strange bright-feathered game we caught!
The hats
O' the fugitives. . .

CARBON.
'Spolia opima!'

ALL [laughing].
Ah! ah! ah!

CUIGY.
He who laid that ambush, 'faith!
Must curse and swear!

BRISSAILLE.
Who was it?

DE GUICHE.
I myself.
[The laughter stops.]
I charged them--work too dirty for my sword,
To punish and chastise a rhymster sot.

[Constrained silence.]

THE CADET [in a low voice, to Cyrano, showing him the beavers].
What do with them? They're full of grease!--a stew?

CYRANO [taking the sword and, with a salute, dropping the hats at
De Guiche's feet].
Sir, pray be good enough to render them
Back to your friends.

DE GUICHE [rising, sharply].
My chair there--quick!--I go!
[To Cyrano passionately]
As to you, sirrah!. . .

VOICE [in the street].
Porters for my lord De Guiche!

DE GUICHE [who has controlled himself--smiling].
Have you read 'Don Quixote'?

CYRANO.
I have!
And doff my hat at th' mad knight-errant's name.

DE GUICHE.
I counsel you to study. . .

A PORTER [appearing at back].
My lord's chair!

DE GUICHE.
. . .The windmill chapter!

CYRANO [bowing].
Chapter the Thirteenth.

DE GUICHE.
For when one tilts 'gainst windmills--it may chance. . .

CYRANO.
Tilt I 'gainst those who change with every breeze?

DE GUICHE.
. . .That windmill sails may sweep you with their arm
Down--in the mire!. . .

CYRANO.
Or upward--to the stars!

[De Guiche goes out, and mounts into his chair. The other lords go
away whispering together. Le Bret goes to the door with them. The
crowd disperses.]

Act II. Scene VIII.

[Cyrano, Le Bret, the cadets, who are eating and drinking at the tables right and left.]

CYRANO [bowing mockingly to those who go out without daring to
salute him].
Gentlemen. . .Gentlemen. . .

LE BRET [coming back, despairingly].
Here's a fine coil!

CYRANO.
Oh! scold away!

LE BRET.
At least, you will agree
That to annihilate each chance of Fate
Exaggerates. . .

CYRANO.
Yes!--I exaggerate!

LE BRET [triumphantly].
Ah!

CYRANO.
But for principle--example too,--
I think 'tis well thus to exaggerate.

LE BRET.
Oh! lay aside that pride of musketeer,
Fortune and glory wait you!. . .

CYRANO.
Ay, and then?. . .
Seek a protector, choose a patron out,
And like the crawling ivy round a tree
That licks the bark to gain the trunk's support,

Climb high by creeping ruse instead of force?
No, grammercy! What! I, like all the rest
Dedicate verse to bankers?--play buffoon
In cringing hope to see, at last, a smile
Not disapproving, on a patron's lips?
Grammercy, no! What! learn to swallow toads?
--With frame aweary climbing stairs?--a skin
Grown grimed and horny,--here, about the knees?
And, acrobat-like, teach my back to bend?--
No, grammercy! Or,--double-faced and sly--
Run with the hare, while hunting with the hounds;
And, oily-tongued, to win the oil of praise,
Flatter the great man to his very nose?
No, grammercy! Steal soft from lap to lap,
--A little great man in a circle small,
Or navigate, with madrigals for sails,
Blown gently windward by old ladies' sighs?
No, grammercy! Bribe kindly editors
To spread abroad my verses? Grammercy!
Or try to be elected as the pope
Of tavern-councils held by imbeciles?
No, grammercy! Toil to gain reputation
By one small sonnet, 'stead of making many?
No, grammercy! Or flatter sorry bunglers?
Be terrorized by every prating paper?
Say ceaselessly, 'Oh, had I but the chance
Of a fair notice in the "Mercury"'!
Grammercy, no! Grow pale, fear, calculate?
Prefer to make a visit to a rhyme?
Seek introductions, draw petitions up?
No, grammercy! and no! and no again! But--sing?
Dream, laugh, go lightly, solitary, free,
With eyes that look straight forward--fearless voice!
To cock your beaver just the way you choose,--
For 'yes' or 'no' show fight, or turn a rhyme!
--To work without one thought of gain or fame,

To realize that journey to the moon!
Never to pen a line that has not sprung
Straight from the heart within. Embracing then
Modesty, say to oneself, 'Good my friend,
Be thou content with flowers,--fruit,--nay, leaves,
But pluck them from no garden but thine own!'
And then, if glory come by chance your way,
To pay no tribute unto Caesar, none,
But keep the merit all your own! In short,
Disdaining tendrils of the parasite,
To be content, if neither oak nor elm--
Not to mount high, perchance, but mount alone!

LE BRET.
Alone, an if you will! But not with hand
'Gainst every man! How in the devil's name
Have you conceived this lunatic idea,
To make foes for yourself at every turn?

CYRANO.
By dint of seeing you at every turn
Make friends,--and fawn upon your frequent friends
With mouth wide smiling, slit from ear to ear!
I pass, still unsaluted, joyfully,
And cry,--What, ho! another enemy?

LE BRET.
Lunacy!

CYRANO.
Well, what if it be my vice,
My pleasure to displease--to love men hate me!
Ah, friend of mine, believe me, I march better
'Neath the cross-fire of glances inimical!
How droll the stains one sees on fine-laced doublets,
From gall of envy, or the poltroon's drivel!

--The enervating friendship which enfolds you
Is like an open-laced Italian collar,
Floating around your neck in woman's fashion;
One is at ease thus,--but less proud the carriage!
The forehead, free from mainstay or coercion,
Bends here, there, everywhere. But I, embracing
Hatred, she lends,--forbidding, stiffly fluted,
The ruff's starched folds that hold the head so rigid;
Each enemy--another fold--a gopher,
Who adds constraint, and adds a ray of glory;
For Hatred, like the ruff worn by the Spanish,
Grips like a vice, but frames you like a halo!

LE BRET [after a silence, taking his arm].
Speak proud aloud, and bitter!--In my ear
Whisper me simply this,--She loves thee not!

CYRANO [vehemently].
Hush!

[Christian has just entered, and mingled with the cadets, who do not
speak to him; he has seated himself at a table, where Lise serves him.]

Act II. Scene IX.

[Cyrano, Le Bret, the cadets, Christian de Neuvillette.]

A CADET [seated at a table, glass in hand].
Cyrano!
[Cyrano turns round.]
The story!

CYRANO.
In its time!

[He goes up on Le Bret's arm. They talk in low voices.]

THE CADET [rising and coming down].
The story of the fray! 'Twill lesson well
[He stops before the table where Christian is seated.]
This timid young apprentice!

CHRISTIAN [raising his head].
'Prentice! Who?

ANOTHER CADET.
This sickly Northern greenhorn!

CHRISTIAN.
Sickly!

FIRST CADET [mockingly].
Hark!
Monsieur de Neuvillette, this in your ear:
There's somewhat here, one no more dares to name,
Than to say 'rope' to one whose sire was hanged!

CHRISTIAN.
What may that be?

ANOTHER CADET [in a terrible voice].
See here!
[He puts his finger three times, mysteriously, on his nose.]
Do you understand?

CHRISTIAN.
Oh! 'tis the. . .

ANOTHER.
Hush! oh, never breathe that word,
Unless you'd reckon with him yonder!

[He points to Cyrano, who is talking with Le Bret.]

ANOTHER [who has meanwhile come up noiselessly to sit on the table—whispering behind him].
Hark!
He put two snuffling men to death, in rage,
For the sole reason they spoke through their nose!

ANOTHER [in a hollow voice, darting on all-fours from under the table, where he had crept].
And if you would not perish in flower o' youth,
--Oh, mention not the fatal cartilage!

ANOTHER [clapping him on the shoulder].
A word? A gesture! For the indiscreet
His handkerchief may prove his winding-sheet!

[Silence. All, with crossed arms, look at Christian. He rises and goes over to Carbon de Castel-Jaloux, who is talking to an officer, and feigns to see nothing.]

CHRISTIAN.
Captain!

CARBON [turning and looking at him from head to foot].
Sir!

CHRISTIAN.
Pray, what skills it best to do
To Southerners who swagger?. . .

CARBON.
Give them proof
That one may be a Northerner, yet brave!

[He turns his back on him.]

CHRISTIAN.

I thank you.

FIRST CADET [to Cyrano].
Now the tale!

ALL.
The tale!

CYRANO [coming toward them].
The tale?. . .
[All bring their stools up, and group round him, listening eagerly.
Christian is astride a chair.]
Well! I went all alone to meet the band.
The moon was shining, clock-like, full i' th' sky,
When, suddenly, some careful clockwright passed
A cloud of cotton-wool across the case
That held this silver watch. And, presto! heigh!
The night was inky black, and all the quays
Were hidden in the murky dark. Gadsooks!
One could see nothing further. . .

CHRISTIAN.
Than one's nose!

[Silence. All slowly rise, looking in terror at Cyrano, who has stopped--
dumbfounded. Pause.]

CYRANO.
Who on God's earth is that?

A CADET [whispering].
It is a man
Who joined to-day.

CYRANO [making a step toward Christian].
To-day?

CARBON [in a low voice].
Yes. . .his name is
The Baron de Neuvil. . .

CYRANO [checking himself].
Good! It is well. . .
[He turns pale, flushes, makes as if to fall on Christian.]
I. . .
[He controls himself.]
What said I?. . .
[With a burst of rage]
MORDIOUS!. . .
[Then continues calmly]
That it was dark.
[Astonishment. The cadets reseat themselves, staring at him.]
On I went, thinking, 'For a knavish cause
I may provoke some great man, some great prince,
Who certainly could break'. . .

CHRISTIAN.
My nose!. . .

[Every one starts up. Christian balances on his chair.]

CYRANO [in a choked voice].
. . .'My teeth!
Who would break my teeth, and I, imprudent-like,
Was poking. . .'

CHRISTIAN.
My nose!. . .

CYRANO.
'My finger,. . .in the crack
Between the tree and bark! He may prove strong
And rap me. . .'

CHRISTIAN.
Over the nose. . .

CYRANO [wiping his forehead].
. . .'O' th' knuckles! Ay,'
But I cried, 'Forward, Gascon! Duty calls!
On, Cyrano!' And thus I ventured on. . .
When, from the shadow, came. . .

CHRISTIAN.
A crack o' th' nose.

CYRANO.
I parry it--find myself. . .

CHRISTIAN.
Nose to nose. . .

CYRANO [bounding on to him].
Heaven and earth!
[All the Gascons leap up to see, but when he is close to Christian he
controls himself and continues.]
. . .With a hundred brawling sots,
Who stank. . .

CHRISTIAN.
A noseful. . .

CYRANO [white, but smiling].
Onions, brandy-cups!
I leapt out, head well down. . .

CHRISTIAN.
Nosing the wind!

CYRANO.

I charge!--gore two, impale one--run him through,
One aims at me--Paf! and I parry. . .

CHRISTIAN.
Pif!

CYRANO [bursting out].
Great God! Out! all of you!

[The cadets rush to the doors.]

FIRST CADET.
The tiger wakes!

CYRANO.
Every man, out! Leave me alone with him!

SECOND CADET.
We shall find him minced fine, minced into hash
In a big pasty!

RAGUENEAU.
I am turning pale,
And curl up, like a napkin, limp and white!

CARBON.
Let us be gone.

ANOTHER.
He will not leave a crumb!

ANOTHER.
I die of fright to think what will pass here!

ANOTHER [shutting door right].
Something too horrible!

[All have gone out by different doors, some by the staircase. Cyrano and Christian are face to face, looking at each other for a moment.]

Act II. Scene X.

[Cyrano, Christian.]

CYRANO.
Embrace me now!

CHRISTIAN.
Sir. . .

CYRANO.
You are brave.

CHRISTIAN.
Oh! but. . .

CYRANO.
Nay, I insist.

CHRISTIAN.
Pray tell me. . .

CYRANO.
Come, embrace! I am her brother.

CHRISTIAN.
Whose brother?

CYRANO.
Hers i' faith! Roxane's!

CHRISTIAN [rushing up to him].
O heavens!

Her brother. . .?

CYRANO.
Cousin—brother!. . .the same thing!

CHRISTIAN.
And she has told you. . .?

CYRANO.
All!

CHRISTIAN.
She loves me? say!

CYRANO.
Maybe!

CHRISTIAN [taking his hands].
How glad I am to meet you, Sir!

CYRANO.
That may be called a sudden sentiment!

CHRISTIAN.
I ask your pardon. . .

CYRANO [looking at him, with his hand on his shoulder].
True, he's fair, the villain!

CHRISTIAN.
Ah, Sir! If you but knew my admiration!. . .

CYRANO.
But all those noses?. . .

CHRISTIAN.

Oh! I take them back!

CYRANO.
Roxane expects a letter.

CHRISTIAN.
Woe the day!

CYRANO.
How?

CHRISTIAN.
I am lost if I but ope my lips!

CYRANO.
Why so?

CHRISTIAN.
I am a fool--could die for shame!

CYRANO.
None is a fool who knows himself a fool.
And you did not attack me like a fool.

CHRISTIAN.
Bah! One finds battle-cry to lead th' assault!
I have a certain military wit,
But, before women, can but hold my tongue.
Their eyes! True, when I pass, their eyes are kind. . .

CYRANO.
And, when you stay, their hearts, methinks, are kinder?

CHRISTIAN.
No! for I am one of those men--tongue-tied,
I know it--who can never tell their love.

CYRANO.

And I, meseems, had Nature been more kind,
More careful, when she fashioned me,--had been
One of those men who well could speak their love!

CHRISTIAN.

Oh, to express one's thoughts with facile grace!. . .

CYRANO.

. . .To be a musketeer, with handsome face!

CHRISTIAN.

Roxane is precieuse. I'm sure to prove
A disappointment to her!

CYRANO [looking at him].

Had I but
Such an interpreter to speak my soul!

CHRISTIAN [with despair].

Eloquence! Where to find it?

CYRANO [abruptly].

That I lend,
If you lend me your handsome victor-charms;
Blended, we make a hero of romance!

CHRISTIAN.

How so?

CYRANO.

Think you you can repeat what things
I daily teach your tongue?

CHRISTIAN.

What do you mean?

CYRANO.
Roxane shall never have a disillusion!
Say, wilt thou that we woo her, double-handed?
Wilt thou that we two woo her, both together?
Feel'st thou, passing from my leather doublet,
Through thy laced doublet, all my soul inspiring?

CHRISTIAN.
But, Cyrano!. . .

CYRANO.
Will you, I say?

CHRISTIAN.
I fear!

CYRANO.
Since, by yourself, you fear to chill her heart,
Will you--to kindle all her heart to flame--
Wed into one my phrases and your lips?

CHRISTIAN.
Your eyes flash!

CYRANO.
Will you?

CHRISTIAN.
Will it please you so?
--Give you such pleasure?

CYRANO [madly].
It!. . .
[Then calmly, business-like]
It would amuse me!
It is an enterprise to tempt a poet.

Will you complete me, and let me complete you?
You march victorious,--I go in your shadow;
Let me be wit for you, be you my beauty!

CHRISTIAN.
The letter, that she waits for even now!
I never can. . .

CYRANO [taking out the letter he had written].
See! Here it is--your letter!

CHRISTIAN.
What?

CYRANO.
Take it! Look, it wants but the address.

CHRISTIAN.
But I. . .

CYRANO.
Fear nothing. Send it. It will suit.

CHRISTIAN.
But have you. . .?

CYRANO.
Oh! We have our pockets full,
We poets, of love-letters, writ to Chloes,
Daphnes--creations of our noddle-heads.
Our lady-loves,--phantasms of our brains,
--Dream-fancies blown into soap-bubbles! Come!
Take it, and change feigned love-words into true;
I breathed my sighs and moans haphazard-wise;
Call all these wandering love-birds home to nest.
You'll see that I was in these lettered lines,

--Eloquent all the more, the less sincere!
--Take it, and make an end!

CHRISTIAN.
Were it not well
To change some words? Written haphazard-wise,
Will it fit Roxane?

CYRANO.
'Twill fit like a glove!

CHRISTIAN.
But. . .

CYRANO.
Ah, credulity of love! Roxane
Will think each word inspired by herself!

CHRISTIAN.
My friend!

[He throws himself into Cyrano's arms. They remain thus.]

Act II. Scene XI.

[Cyrano, Christian, the Gascons, the musketeer, Lise.]

A CADET [half opening the door].
Naught here!. . .The silence of the grave!
I dare not look. . .
[He puts his head in.]
Why?. . .

ALL THE CADETS [entering, and seeing Cyrano and Christian embracing].
Oh!. . .

A CADET.
This passes all!

[Consternation.]

THE MUSKETEER [mockingly].
Ho, ho!. . .

CARBON.
Our demon has become a saint?
Struck on one nostril--lo! he turns the other!

MUSKETEER.
Then we may speak about his nose, henceforth!. . .
[Calling to Lise, boastfully]
--Ah, Lise, see here!
[Sniffing ostentatiously]
O heavens!. . .what a stink!. . .
[Going up to Cyrano]
You, sir, without a doubt have sniffed it up!
--What is the smell I notice here?

CYRANO [cuffing his head].
Clove-heads.

[General delight. The cadets have found the old Cyrano again! They
turn somersaults.]

[Curtain.]

ACT III

Roxane's Kiss.

A small square in the old Marais. Old houses. A perspective of little streets. On the right Roxane's house and the wall of her garden overhung with thick foliage. Window and balcony over the door. A bench in front.

From the bench and the stones jutting out of the wall it is easy to climb to the balcony. In front of an old house in the same style of brick and stone. The knocker of this door is bandaged with linen like a sore thumb.

At the rising of the curtain the duenna is seated on the bench.

The window on Roxane's balcony is wide open.

Ragueneau is standing near the door in a sort of livery. He has just finished relating something to the duenna, and is wiping his eyes.

Act III. Scene I.

[Ragueneau, the duenna. Then Roxane, Cyrano, and two pages.]

RAGUENEAU.
--And then, off she went, with a musketeer! Deserted and ruined too, I
would make an end of all, and so hanged myself. My last breath
was drawn:--
then in comes Monsieur de Bergerac! He cuts me down, and begs his
cousin to take me for her steward.

THE DUENNA.
Well, but how came it about that you were thus ruined?

RAGUENEAU.
Oh! Lise loved the warriors, and I loved the poets! What cakes there
were that Apollo chanced to leave were quickly snapped up by Mars.
Thus ruin was not long a-coming.

THE DUENNA [rising, and calling up to the open window].
Roxane, are you ready? They wait for us!

ROXANE'S VOICE [from the window].
I will but put me on a cloak!

THE DUENNA [to Ragueneau, showing him the door opposite].
They wait us there opposite, at Clomire's house. She receives them all
there to-day--the precieuses, the poets; they read a discourse on the
Tender Passion.

RAGUENEAU.
The Tender Passion?

THE DUENNA [in a mincing voice].
Ay, indeed!
[Calling up to the window]
Roxane, an you come not down quickly, we shall miss the discourse on
the Tender Passion!

ROXANE'S VOICE.
I come! I come!

[A sound of stringed instruments approaching.]

CYRANO'S VOICE [behind the scenes, singing].
La, la, la, la!

THE DUENNA [surprised].
They serenade us?

CYRANO [followed by two pages with arch-lutes].
I tell you they are demi-semi-quavers, demi-semi-fool!

FIRST PAGE [ironically].
You know then, Sir, to distinguish between semi-quavers and demi-semi-quavers?

CYRANO.
Is not every disciple of Gassendi a musician?

THE PAGE [playing and singing].
La, la!

CYRANO [snatching the lute from him, and going on with the phrase].
In proof of which, I can continue! La, la, la, la!

ROXANE [appearing on the balcony].
What? 'Tis you?

CYRANO [going on with the air, and singing to it].
'Tis I, who come to serenade your lilies, and pay my devoir to your ro-o-oses!

ROXANE.

I am coming down!

[She leaves the balcony.]

THE DUENNA [pointing to the pages].
How come these two virtuosi here?

CYRANO.
'Tis for a wager I won of D'Assoucy. We were disputing a nice point in
grammar; contradictions raged hotly--"'Tis so!' 'Nay, 'tis so!' when
suddenly he shows me these two long-shanks, whom he takes about
with him as an escort, and who are skillful in scratching lute-strings
with their skinny claws! 'I will wager you a day's music,' says he!--And
lost it! Thus, see you, till Phoebus' chariot starts once again, these lute-
twangers are at my heels, seeing all I do, hearing all I say, and accompa-
nying all with melody. 'Twas pleasant at the first, but i' faith, I begin to
weary of it already!
[To the musicians]
Ho there! go serenade Montfleury for me! Play a dance to him!
[The pages go toward the door. To the duenna]
I have come, as is my wont, nightly, to ask Roxane whether. . .
[To the pages, who are going out]
Play a long time,--and play out of tune!
[To the duenna]
. . .Whether her soul's elected is ever the same, ever faultless!

ROXANE [coming out of the house].
Ah! How handsome he is, how brilliant a wit! And--how well I
love him!

CYRANO [smiling].
Christian has so brilliant a wit?

ROXANE.
Brighter than even your own, cousin!

CYRANO.
Be it so, with all my heart!

ROXANE.
Ah! methinks 'twere impossible that there could breathe a man on this
earth skilled to say as sweetly as he all the pretty nothings that mean
so much--that mean all! At times his mind seems far away, the Muse
says naught--and then, presto! he speaks--bewitchingly! enchantingly!

CYRANO [incredulously].
No, no!

ROXANE.
Fie! That is ill said! But lo! men are ever thus! Because he is fair to
see, you would have it that he must be dull of speech.

CYRANO.
He hath an eloquent tongue in telling his love?

ROXANE.
In telling his love? why, 'tis not simple telling, 'tis dissertation, 'tis
analysis!

CYRANO.
How is he with the pen?

ROXANE.
Still better! Listen,--here:--
[Reciting]
'The more of my poor heart you take
The larger grows my heart!'
[Triumphantly to Cyrano]
How like you those lines?

CYRANO.
Pooh!

ROXANE.
And thus it goes on. . .
'And, since some target I must show
For Cupid's cruel dart,
Oh, if mine own you deign to keep,
Then give me your sweet heart!'

CYRANO.
Lord! first he has too much, then anon not enough! How much heart
does the fellow want?

ROXANE.
You would vex a saint!. . .But 'tis your jealousy.

CYRANO [starting].
What mean you?

ROXANE.
Ay, your poet's jealousy! Hark now, if this again be not tender-sweet?--
'My heart to yours sounds but one cry:
If kisses fast could flee
By letter, then with your sweet lips
My letters read should be!
If kisses could be writ with ink,
If kisses fast could flee!'

CYRANO [smiling approvingly in spite of himself].
Ha! those last lines are,--hm!. . .hm!. . .
[Correcting himself--contemptuously]
--They are paltry enough!

ROXANE.
And this. . .

CYRANO [enchanted].
Then you have his letters by heart?

ROXANE.
Every one of them!

CYRANO.
By all oaths that can be sworn,--'tis flattering!

ROXANE.
They are the lines of a master!

CYRANO [modestly].
Come, nay. . .a master?. . .

ROXANE.
Ay, I say it--a master!

CYRANO.
Good--be it so.

THE DUENNA [coming down quickly].
Here comes Monsieur de Guiche!
[To Cyrano, pushing him toward the house]
In with you! 'twere best he see you not; it might perchance put him on
the scent. . .

ROXANE [to Cyrano].
Ay, of my own dear secret! He loves me, and is powerful, and, if he
knew, then all were lost! Marry! he could well deal a deathblow to
my love!

CYRANO [entering the house].
Good! good!

[De Guiche appears.]

Act III. Scene II.

[Roxane, De Guiche, the duenna standing a little way off.]

ROXANE [courtesying to De Guiche].
I was going out.

DE GUICHE.
I come to take my leave.

ROXANE.
Whither go you?

DE GUICHE.
To the war.

ROXANE.
Ah!

DE GUICHE.
Ay, to-night.

ROXANE.
Oh!

DE GUICHE.
I am ordered away. We are to besiege Arras.

ROXANE.
Ah--to besiege?. . .

DE GUICHE.
Ay. My going moves you not, meseems.

ROXANE.
Nay. . .

DE GUICHE.

I am grieved to the core of the heart. Shall I again behold
you?. . .When?
I know not. Heard you that I am named commander?. . .

ROXANE [indifferently].
Bravo!

DE GUICHE.
Of the Guards regiment.

ROXANE [startled].
What! the Guards?

DE GUICHE.
Ay, where serves your cousin, the swaggering boaster. I will find a way
to revenge myself on him at Arras.

ROXANE [choking].
What mean you? The Guards go to Arras?

DE GUICHE [laughing].
Bethink you, is it not my own regiment?

ROXANE [falling seated on the bench--aside].
Christian!

DE GUICHE.
What ails you?

ROXANE [moved deeply].
Oh--I am in despair! The man one loves!--at the war!

DE GUICHE [surprised and delighted].
You say such sweet words to me! 'Tis the first time!--and just when I
must quit you!

ROXANE [collected, and fanning herself].
Thus,--you would fain revenge your grudge against my cousin?

DE GUICHE.
My fair lady is on his side?

ROXANE.
Nay,--against him!

DE GUICHE.
Do you see him often?

ROXANE.
But very rarely.

DE GUICHE.
He is ever to be met now in company with one of the cadets,. . .one
New--villen--viller--

ROXANE.
Of high stature?

DE GUICHE.
Fair-haired!

ROXANE.
Ay, a red-headed fellow!

DE GUICHE.
Handsome!. . .

ROXANE.
Tut!

DE GUICHE.
But dull-witted.

ROXANE.
One would think so, to look at him!
[Changing her tone]
How mean you to play your revenge on Cyrano? Perchance you think
to put him i' the thick of the shots? Nay, believe me, that were a poor
vengeance--he would love such a post better than aught else! I know
the way to wound his pride far more keenly!

DE GUICHE.
What then? Tell. . .

ROXANE.
If, when the regiment march to Arras, he were left here with his
beloved boon companions, the Cadets, to sit with crossed arms so long
as the war lasted! There is your method, would you enrage a man of his
kind; cheat him of his chance of mortal danger, and you punish him
right fiercely.

DE GUICHE [coming nearer].
O woman! woman! Who but a woman had e'er devised so subtle
a trick?

ROXANE.
See you not how he will eat out his heart, while his friends gnaw their
thick fists for that they are deprived of the battle? So are you best
avenged.

DE GUICHE.
You love me, then, a little?
[She smiles.]
I would fain--seeing you thus espouse my cause, Roxane--believe it a
proof of love!

ROXANE.
'Tis a proof of love!

DE GUICHE [showing some sealed papers].
Here are the marching orders; they will be sent instantly to each
company--except--
[He detaches one.]
--This one! 'Tis that of the Cadets.
[He puts it in his pocket.]
This I keep.
[Laughing]
Ha! ha! ha! Cyrano! His love of battle!. . .So you can play tricks on
people?. . .you, of all ladies!

ROXANE.
Sometimes!

DE GUICHE [coming close to her].
Oh! how I love you!--to distraction! Listen! To-night--true, I ought to
start--but--how leave you now that I feel your heart is touched! Hard
by, in the Rue d'Orleans, is a convent founded by Father Athanasius,
the syndic of the Capuchins. True that no layman may enter--but--I
can settle that with the good Fathers! Their habit sleeves are wide
enough to hide me in. 'Tis they who serve Richelieu's private chapel:
and from respect to the uncle, fear the nephew. All will deem me gone.
I will come to you, masked. Give me leave to wait till tomorrow, sweet
Lady Fanciful!

ROXANE.
But, of this be rumored, your glory. . .

DE GUICHE.
Bah!

ROXANE.
But the siege--Arras. . .

DE GUICHE.
'Twill take its chance. Grant but permission.

ROXANE.
No!

DE GUICHE.
Give me leave!

ROXANE [tenderly].
It were my duty to forbid you!

DE GUICHE.
Ah!

ROXANE.
You must go!
[Aside]
Christian stays here.
[Aloud]
I would have you heroic--Antoine!

DE GUICHE.
O heavenly word! You love, then, him?. . .

ROXANE.
. . .For whom I trembled.

DE GUICHE [in an ecstasy].
Ah! I go then!
[He kisses her hand.]
Are you content?

ROXANE.
Yes, my friend!

[He goes out.]

THE DUENNA [making behind his back a mocking courtesy].

Yes, my friend!

ROXANE [to the duenna].
Not a word of what I have done. Cyrano would never pardon me for
stealing his fighting from him!
[She calls toward the house.]
Cousin!

Act III. Scene III.

[Roxane, The duenna, Cyrano.]

ROXANE.
We are going to Clomire's house.
[She points to the door opposite.]
Alcandre and Lysimon are to discourse!

THE DUENNA [putting her little finger in her ear].
Yes! But my little finger tells me we shall miss them.

CYRANO.
'Twere a pity to miss such apes!

[They have come to Clomire's door.]

THE DUENNA.
Oh, see! The knocker is muffled up!
[Speaking to the knocker]
So they have gagged that metal tongue of yours, little noisy one, lest it
should disturb the fine orators!

[She lifts it carefully and knocks with precaution.]

ROXANE [seeing that the door opens].
Let us enter!
[On the threshold, to Cyrano]

If Christian comes, as I feel sure he will, bid him wait for me!

CYRANO [quickly, as she is going in].
Listen!
[She turns]
What mean you to question him on, as is your wont, to-night?

ROXANE.
Oh--

CYRANO [eagerly].
Well, say.

ROXANE.
But you will be mute?

CYRANO.
Mute as a fish.

ROXANE.
I shall not question him at all, but say: Give rein to your fancy! Prepare not your speeches,--but speak the thoughts as they come! Speak to me of love, and speak splendidly!

CYRANO [smiling].
Very good!

ROXANE.
But secret!. . .

CYRANO.
Secret.

ROXANE.
Not a word!

[She enters and shuts the door.]

CYRANO [when the door is shut, bowing to her].
A thousand thanks!

[The door opens again, and Roxane puts her head out.]

ROXANE.
Lest he prepare himself!

CYRANO.
The devil!--no, no!

BOTH TOGETHER.
Secret.

[The door shuts.]

CYRANO [calling].
Christian!

Act III. Scene IV.

[Cyrano, Christian.]

CYRANO.
I know all that is needful. Here's occasion
For you to deck yourself with glory. Come,
Lose no time; put away those sulky looks,
Come to your house with me, I'll teach you. . .

CHRISTIAN.
No!

CYRANO.
Why?

CHRISTIAN.
I will wait for Roxane here.

CYRANO.
How? Crazy?
Come quick with me and learn. . .

CHRISTIAN.
No, no! I say.
I am aweary of these borrowed letters,
--Borrowed love-makings! Thus to act a part,
And tremble all the time!--'Twas well enough
At the beginning!--Now I know she loves!
I fear no longer!--I will speak myself.

CYRANO.
Mercy!

CHRISTIAN.
And how know you I cannot speak?--
I am not such a fool when all is said!
I've by your lessons profited. You'll see
I shall know how to speak alone! The devil!
I know at least to clasp her in my arms!
[Seeing Roxane come out from Clomire's house]
--It is she! Cyrano, no!--Leave me not!

CYRANO [bowing].
Speak for yourself, my friend, and take your chance.

[He disappears behind the garden wall.]

Act III. Scene V.

[Christian, Roxane, the duenna.]

ROXANE [coming out of Clomire's house, with a company of friends, whom she leaves. Bows and good-byes].
Barthenoide!--Alcandre!--Gremione!--

THE DUENNA [bitterly disappointed].
We've missed the speech upon the Tender Passion!

[Goes into Roxane's house.]

ROXANE [still bowing].
Urimedonte--adieu!
[All bow to Roxane and to each other, and then separate, going up different streets. Roxane suddenly seeing Christian]
You!
[She goes to him.]
Evening falls.
Let's sit. Speak on. I listen.

CHRISTIAN [sits by her on the bench. A silence].
Oh! I love you!

ROXANE [shutting her eyes].
Ay, speak to me of love.

CHRISTIAN.
I love thee!

ROXANE.
That's
The theme! But vary it.

CHRISTIAN.
I. . .

ROXANE.
Vary it!

CHRISTIAN.
I love you so!

ROXANE.
Oh! without doubt!--and then?. . .

CHRISTIAN.
And then--I should be--oh!--so glad--so glad
If you would love me!--Roxane, tell me so!

ROXANE [with a little grimace].
I hoped for cream,--you give me gruel! Say
How love possesses you?

CHRISTIAN.
Oh utterly!

ROXANE.
Come, come!. . .unknot those tangled sentiments!

CHRISTIAN.
Your throat I'd kiss it!

ROXANE.
Christian!

CHRISTIAN.
I love thee!

ROXANE [half-rising].
Again!

CHRISTIAN [eagerly, detaining her].
No, no! I love thee not!

ROXANE [reseating herself].

'Tis well!

CHRISTIAN.
But I adore thee!

ROXANE [rising, and going further off].
Oh!

CHRISTIAN.
I am grown stupid!

ROXANE [dryly].
And that displeases me, almost as much
As 'twould displease me if you grew ill-favored.

CHRISTIAN.
But. . .

ROXANE.
Rally your poor eloquence that's flown!

CHRISTIAN.
I. . .

ROXANE.
Yes, you love me, that I know. Adieu.

[She goes toward her house.]

CHRISTIAN.
Oh, go not yet! I'd tell you--

ROXANE [opening the door].
You adore me?
I've heard it very oft. No!--Go away!

CHRISTIAN.
But I would fain. . .

[She shuts the door in his face.]

CYRANO [who has re-entered unseen].
I' faith! It is successful!

Act III. Scene VI.

[Christian, Cyrano, two pages.]

CHRISTIAN.
Come to my aid!

CYRANO.
Not I!

CHRISTIAN.
But I shall die,
Unless at once I win back her fair favor.

CYRANO.
And how can I, at once, i' th' devil's name,
Lesson you in. . .

CHRISTIAN [seizing his arm].
Oh, she is there!

[The window of the balcony is now lighted up.]

CYRANO [moved].
Her window!

CHRISTIAN.
Oh! I shall die!

CYRANO.
Speak lower!

CHRISTIAN [in a whisper].
I shall die!

CYRANO.
The night is dark. . .

CHRISTIAN.
Well!

CYRANO.
All can be repaired.
Although you merit not. Stand there, poor wretch!
Fronting the balcony! I'll go beneath
And prompt your words to you. . .

CHRISTIAN.
But. . .

CYRANO.
Hold your tongue!

THE PAGES [reappearing at back--to Cyrano].
Ho!

CYRANO.
Hush!

[He signs to them to speak softly.]

FIRST PAGE [in a low voice].
We've played the serenade you bade
To Montfleury!

CYRANO [quickly, in a low voice].
Go! lurk in ambush there,
One at this street corner, and one at that;
And if a passer-by should here intrude,
Play you a tune!

SECOND PAGE.
What tune, Sir Gassendist?

CYRANO.
Gay, if a woman comes,--for a man, sad!
[The pages disappear, one at each street corner. To Christian]
Call her!

CHRISTIAN.
Roxane!

CYRANO [picking up stones and throwing them at the window].
Some pebbles! wait awhile!

ROXANE [half-opening the casement].
Who calls me?

CHRISTIAN.
I!

ROXANE.
Who's that?

CHRISTIAN.
Christian!

ROXANE [disdainfully].
Oh! you?

CHRISTIAN.

I would speak with you.

CYRANO [under the balcony--to Christian].
Good. Speak soft and low.

ROXANE.
No, you speak stupidly!

CHRISTIAN.
Oh, pity me!

ROXANE.
No! you love me no more!

CHRISTIAN [prompted by Cyrano].
You say--Great Heaven!
I love no more?--when--I--love more and more!

ROXANE [who was about to shut the casement, pausing].
Hold! 'tis a trifle better! ay, a trifle!

CHRISTIAN [same play].
Love grew apace, rocked by the anxious beating. . .
Of this poor heart, which the cruel wanton boy. . .
Took for a cradle!

ROXANE [coming out on to the balcony].
That is better! But
An if you deem that Cupid be so cruel
You should have stifled baby-love in's cradle!

CHRISTIAN [same play].
Ah, Madame, I assayed, but all in vain
This. . .new-born babe is a young. . .Hercules!

ROXANE.

Still better!

CHRISTIAN [same play].
Thus he strangled in my heart
The. . .serpents twain, of. . .Pride. . .and Doubt!

ROXANE [leaning over the balcony].
Well said!
--But why so faltering? Has mental palsy
Seized on your faculty imaginative?

CYRANO [drawing Christian under the balcony, and slipping into his place].
Give place! This waxes critical!. . .

ROXANE.
To-day. . .
Your words are hesitating.

CYRANO [imitating Christian--in a whisper].
Night has come. . .
In the dusk they grope their way to find your ear.

ROXANE.
But my words find no such impediment.

CYRANO.
They find their way at once? Small wonder that!
For 'tis within my heart they find their home;
Bethink how large my heart, how small your ear!
And,--from fair heights descending, words fall fast,
But mine must mount, Madame, and that takes time!

ROXANE.
Meseems that your last words have learned to climb.

CYRANO.
With practice such gymnastic grows less hard!

ROXANE.
In truth, I seem to speak from distant heights!

CYRANO.
True, far above; at such a height 'twere death
If a hard word from you fell on my heart.

ROXANE [moving].
I will come down. . .

CYRANO [hastily].
No!

ROXANE [showing him the bench under the balcony].
Mount then on the bench!

CYRANO [starting back alarmed].
No!

ROXANE.
How, you will not?

CYRANO [more and more moved].
Stay awhile! 'Tis sweet,. . .
The rare occasion, when our hearts can speak
Our selves unseen, unseeing!

ROXANE.
Why--unseen?

CYRANO.
Ay, it is sweet! Half hidden,--half revealed--
You see the dark folds of my shrouding cloak,

And I, the glimmering whiteness of your dress:
I but a shadow--you a radiance fair!
Know you what such a moment holds for me?
If ever I were eloquent. . .

ROXANE.
You were!

CYRANO.
Yet never till to-night my speech has sprung
Straight from my heart as now it springs.

ROXANE.
Why not?

CYRANO.
Till now I spoke haphazard. . .

ROXANE.
What?

CYRANO.
Your eyes
Have beams that turn men dizzy!--But to-night
Methinks I shall find speech for the first time!

ROXANE.
'Tis true, your voice rings with a tone that's new.

CYRANO [coming nearer, passionately].
Ay, a new tone! In the tender, sheltering dusk
I dare to be myself for once,--at last!
[He stops, falters.]
What say I? I know not!--Oh, pardon me--
It thrills me,--'tis so sweet, so novel. . .

ROXANE.
How?
So novel?

CYRANO [off his balance, trying to find the thread of his sentence].
Ay,--to be at last sincere;
Till now, my chilled heart, fearing to be mocked. . .

ROXANE.
Mocked, and for what?

CYRANO.
For its mad beating!--Ay,
My heart has clothed itself with witty words,
To shroud itself from curious eyes:--impelled
At times to aim at a star, I stay my hand,
And, fearing ridicule,--cull a wild flower!

ROXANE.
A wild flower's sweet.

CYRANO.
Ay, but to-night--the star!

ROXANE.
Oh! never have you spoken thus before!

CYRANO.
If, leaving Cupid's arrows, quivers, torches,
We turned to seek for sweeter--fresher things!
Instead of sipping in a pygmy glass
Dull fashionable waters,--did we try
How the soul slakes its thirst in fearless draught
By drinking from the river's flooding brim!

ROXANE.

But wit?. . .

CYRANO.
If I have used it to arrest you
At the first starting,--now, 'twould be an outrage,
An insult--to the perfumed Night--to Nature--
To speak fine words that garnish vain love-letters!
Look up but at her stars! The quiet Heaven
Will ease our hearts of all things artificial;
I fear lest, 'midst the alchemy we're skilled in
The truth of sentiment dissolve and vanish,--
The soul exhausted by these empty pastimes,
The gain of fine things be the loss of all things!

ROXANE.
But wit? I say. . .

CYRANO.
In love 'tis crime,--'tis hateful!
Turning frank loving into subtle fencing!
At last the moment comes, inevitable,--
--Oh, woe for those who never know that moment!
When feeling love exists in us, ennobling,
Each well-weighed word is futile and soul-saddening!

ROXANE.
Well, if that moment's come for us--suppose it!
What words would serve you?

CYRANO.
All, all, all, whatever
That came to me, e'en as they came, I'd fling them
In a wild cluster, not a careful bouquet.
I love thee! I am mad! I love, I stifle!
Thy name is in my heart as in a sheep-bell,
And as I ever tremble, thinking of thee,

Ever the bell shakes, ever thy name ringeth!
All things of thine I mind, for I love all things;
I know that last year on the twelfth of May-month,
To walk abroad, one day you changed your hair-plaits!
I am so used to take your hair for daylight
That,--like as when the eye stares on the sun's disk,
One sees long after a red blot on all things--
So, when I quit thy beams, my dazzled vision
Sees upon all things a blonde stain imprinted.

ROXANE [agitated].
Why, this is love indeed!. . .

CYRANO.
Ay, true, the feeling
Which fills me, terrible and jealous, truly
Love,--which is ever sad amid its transports!
Love,--and yet, strangely, not a selfish passion!
I for your joy would gladly lay mine own down,
--E'en though you never were to know it,--never!
--If but at times I might--far off and lonely,--
Hear some gay echo of the joy I bought you!
Each glance of thine awakes in me a virtue,--
A novel, unknown valor. Dost begin, sweet,
To understand? So late, dost understand me?
Feel'st thou my soul, here, through the darkness mounting?
Too fair the night! Too fair, too fair the moment!
That I should speak thus, and that you should hearken!
Too fair! In moments when my hopes rose proudest,
I never hoped such guerdon. Naught is left me
But to die now! Have words of mine the power
To make you tremble,--throned there in the branches?
Ay, like a leaf among the leaves, you tremble!
You tremble! For I feel,--an if you will it,
Or will it not,--your hand's beloved trembling
Thrill through the branches, down your sprays of jasmine!

[He kisses passionately one of the hanging tendrils.]

ROXANE.
Ay! I am trembling, weeping!--I am thine!
Thou hast conquered all of me!

CYRANO.
Then let death come!
'Tis I, 'tis I myself, who conquered thee!
One thing, but one, I dare to ask--

CHRISTIAN [under the balcony].
A kiss!

ROXANE [drawing back].
What?

CYRANO.
Oh!

ROXANE.
You ask. . .?

CYRANO.
I. . .
[To Christian, whispering]
Fool! you go too quick!

CHRISTIAN.
Since she is moved thus--I will profit by it!

CYRANO [to Roxane].
My words sprang thoughtlessly, but now I see--
Shame on me!--I was too presumptuous.

ROXANE [a little chilled].

How quickly you withdraw.

CYRANO.
Yes, I withdraw
Without withdrawing! Hurt I modesty?
If so--the kiss I asked--oh, grant it not.

CHRISTIAN [to Cyrano, pulling him by his cloak].
Why?

CYRANO.
Silence, Christian! Hush!

ROXANE [leaning over].
What whisper you?

CYRANO.
I chid myself for my too bold advances;
Said, 'Silence, Christian!'
[The lutes begin to play.]
Hark! Wait awhile,. . .
Steps come!
[Roxane shuts the window. Cyrano listens to the lutes, one of which
plays a merry, the other a melancholy, tune.]
Why, they play sad--then gay--then sad! What? Neither man nor
woman?--oh! a monk!

[Enter a capuchin friar, with a lantern. He goes from house to house,
looking at every door.]

Act III. Scene VII.

[Cyrano, Christian, a capuchin friar.]

CYRANO [to the friar].
What do you, playing at Diogenes?

THE FRIAR.
I seek the house of Madame. . .

CHRISTIAN.
Oh! plague take him!

THE FRIAR.
Madeleine Robin. . .

CHRISTIAN.
What would he?. . .

CYRANO [pointing to a street at the back].
This way!
Straight on. . .

THE FRIAR.
I thank you, and, in your intention
Will tell my rosary to its last bead.

[He goes out.]

CYRANO.
Good luck! My blessings rest upon your cowl!

[He goes back to Christian.]

Act III. Scene VIII.

[Cyrano, Christian.]

CHRISTIAN.
Oh! win for me that kiss. . .

CYRANO.
No!

CHRISTIAN.
Soon or late!...

CYRANO.
'Tis true! The moment of intoxication--
Of madness,--when your mouths are sure to meet
Thanks to your fair mustache--and her rose lips!
[To himself]
I'd fainer it should come thanks to...

[A sound of shutters reopening. Christian goes in again under the balcony.]

Act III. Scene IX.

[Cyrano, Christian, Roxane.]

ROXANE [coming out on the balcony].
Still there?
We spoke of a...

CYRANO.
A kiss! The word is sweet.
I see not why your lip should shrink from it;
If the word burns it,--what would the kiss do?
Oh! let it not your bashfulness affright;
Have you not, all this time, insensibly,
Left badinage aside, and unalarmed
Glided from smile to sigh,--from sigh to weeping?
Glide gently, imperceptibly, still onward--
From tear to kiss,--a moment's thrill!--a heartbeat!

ROXANE.
Hush! hush!

CYRANO.

A kiss, when all is said,--what is it?
An oath that's ratified,--a sealed promise,
A heart's avowal claiming confirmation,--
A rose-dot on the 'i' of 'adoration,'--
A secret that to mouth, not ear, is whispered,--
Brush of a bee's wing, that makes time eternal,--
Communion perfumed like the spring's wild flowers,--
The heart's relieving in the heart's outbreathing,
When to the lips the soul's flood rises, brimming!

ROXANE.
Hush! hush!

CYRANO.
A kiss, Madame, is honorable:
The Queen of France, to a most favored lord
Did grant a kiss--the Queen herself!

ROXANE.
What then?

CYRANO [speaking more warmly].
Buckingham suffered dumbly,--so have I,--
Adored his Queen, as loyally as I,--
Was sad, but faithful,--so am I. . .

ROXANE.
And you
Are fair as Buckingham!

CYRANO [aside--suddenly cooled].
True,--I forgot!

ROXANE.
Must I then bid thee mount to cull this flower?

CYRANO [pushing Christian toward the balcony].
Mount!

ROXANE.
This heart-breathing!. . .

CYRANO.
Mount!

ROXANE.
This brush of bee's wing!. . .

CYRANO.
Mount!

CHRISTIAN [hesitating].
But I feel now, as though 'twere ill done!

ROXANE.
This moment infinite!. . .

CYRANO [still pushing him].
Come, blockhead, mount!

[Christian springs forward, and by means of the bench, the branches,
     and the pillars, climbs to the balcony and strides over it.]

CHRISTIAN.
Ah, Roxane!

[He takes her in his arms, and bends over her lips.]

CYRANO:
Aie! Strange pain that wrings my heart!
The kiss, love's feast, so near! I, Lazarus,
Lie at the gate in darkness. Yet to me

Falls still a crumb or two from the rich man's board--
Ay, 'tis my heart receives thee, Roxane--mine!
For on the lips you press you kiss as well
The words I spoke just now!--my words--my words!
[The lutes play.]
A sad air,--a gay air: the monk!
[He begins to run as if he came from a long way off, and cries out.]
Hola!

ROXANE.
Who is it?

CYRANO.
I--I was but passing by. . .
Is Christian there?

CHRISTIAN [astonished].
Cyrano!

ROXANE.
Good-day, cousin!

CYRANO.
Cousin, good-day!

ROXANE.
I'm coming!

 [She disappears into the house. At the back re-enter the friar.]

CHRISTIAN [seeing him].
Back again!

    [He follows Roxane.]

Act III. Scene X.

[Cyrano, Christian, Roxane, the friar, Ragueneau.]

THE FRIAR.
'Tis here,--I'm sure of it--Madame Madeleine Robin.

CYRANO.
Why, you said Ro-LIN.

THE FRIAR.
No, not I.
B,I,N,BIN!

ROXANE [appearing on the threshold, followed by Ragueneau, who carries a lantern, and Christian].
What is't?

THE FRIAR.
A letter.

CHRISTIAN.
What?

THE FRIAR [to Roxane].
Oh, it can boot but a holy business!
'Tis from a worthy lord. . .

ROXANE [to Christian].
De Guiche!

CHRISTIAN.
He dares. . .

ROXANE.
Oh, he will not importune me forever!
[Unsealing the letter]
I love you,--therefore--

[She reads in a low voice by the aid of Ragueneau's lantern.]
'Lady,
The drums beat;
My regiment buckles its harness on
And starts; but I,--they deem me gone before--
But I stay. I have dared to disobey
Your mandate. I am here in convent walls.
I come to you to-night. By this poor monk--
A simple fool who knows not what he bears--
I send this missive to apprise your ear.
Your lips erewhile have smiled on me, too sweet:
I go not ere I've seen them once again!
I would be private; send each soul away,
Receive alone him,--whose great boldness you
Have deigned, I hope, to pardon, ere he asks,--
He who is ever your--et cetera.'
[To the monk]
Father, this is the matter of the letter:--
[All come near her, and she reads aloud]
'Lady,
The Cardinal's wish is law; albeit
It be to you unwelcome. For this cause
I send these lines--to your fair ear addressed--
By a holy man, discreet, intelligent:
It is our will that you receive from him,
In your own house, the marriage
[She turns the page.]
benediction
Straightway, this night. Unknown to all the world
Christian becomes your husband. Him we send.
He is abhorrent to your choice. Let be.
Resign yourself, and this obedience
Will be by Heaven well recompensed. Receive,
Fair lady, all assurance of respect,
From him who ever was, and still remains,
Your humble and obliged--et cetera.'

THE FRIAR [with great delight].
O worthy lord! I knew naught was to fear;
It could be but holy business!

ROXANE [to Christian, in a low voice].
Am I not apt at reading letters?

CHRISTIAN.
Hum!

ROXANE [aloud, with despair].
But this is horrible!

THE FRIAR [who has turned his lantern on Cyrano].
'Tis you?

CHRISTIAN.
'Tis I!

THE FRIAR [turning the light on to him, and as if a doubt struck him
on seeing his beauty].
But. . .

ROXANE [quickly].
I have overlooked the postscript--see:--
'Give twenty pistoles for the Convent.'

THE FRIAR.
. . .Oh!
Most worthy lord!
[To Roxane]
Submit you?

ROXANE [with a martyr's look].
I submit!
[While Ragueneau opens the door, and Christian invites the friar to

enter, she whispers to Cyrano.]
Oh, keep De Guiche at bay! He will be here!
Let him not enter till. . .

CYRANO.
I understand!
[To the friar]
What time need you to tie the marriage-knot?

THE FRIAR.
A quarter of an hour.

CYRANO [pushing them all toward the house].
Go! I stay.

ROXANE [to Christian].
Come!. . .

[They enter.]

CYRANO.
Now, how to detain De Guiche so long?
[He jumps on the bench, climbs to the balcony by the wall.]
Come!. . .up I go!. . .I have my plan!. . .
[The lutes begin to play a very sad air.]
What, ho!
[The tremolo grows more and more weird.]
It is a man! ay! 'tis a man this time!
[He is on the balcony, pulls his hat over his eyes, takes off his sword,
wraps himself in his cloak, then leans over.]
'Tis not too high!
[He strides across the balcony, and drawing to him a long branch of
one of the trees that are by the garden wall, he hangs on to it with
both hands, ready to let himself fall.]
I'll shake this atmosphere!

Act III. Scene XI.

[Cyrano, De Guiche.]

DE GUICHE [who enters, masked, feeling his way in the dark].
What can that cursed Friar be about?

CYRANO.
The devil!. . .If he knows my voice!
[Letting go with one hand, he pretends to turn an invisible key.
Solemnly]
Cric! Crac!
Assume thou, Cyrano, to serve the turn,
The accent of thy native Bergerac!. . .

DE GUICHE [looking at the house].
'Tis there. I see dim,--this mask hinders me!
[He is about to enter, when Cyrano leaps from the balcony, holding on
to the branch, which bends, dropping him between the door and De
Guiche; he pretends to fall heavily, as from a great height, and lies flat
on the ground, motionless, as if stunned. De Guiche starts back.]
What's this?
[When he looks up, the branch has sprung back into its place. He sees
only the sky, and is lost in amazement.]
Where fell that man from?

CYRANO [sitting up, and speaking with a Gascon accent].
From the moon!

DE GUICHE.
From?. . .

CYRANO [in a dreamy voice].
What's o'clock?

DE GUICHE.

He's lost his mind, for sure!

CYRANO.
What hour? What country this? What month? What day?

DE GUICHE.
But. . .

CYRANO.
I am stupefied!

DE GUICHE.
Sir!

CYRANO.
Like a bomb
I fell from the moon!

DE GUICHE [impatiently].
Come now!

CYRANO [rising, in a terrible voice].
I say,--the moon!

DE GUICHE [recoiling].
Good, good! let it be so!. . .He's raving mad!

CYRANO [walking up to him].
I say from the moon! I mean no metaphor!. . .

DE GUICHE.
But. . .

CYRANO.
Was't a hundred years--a minute, since?
--I cannot guess what time that fall embraced!--

That I was in that saffron-colored ball?

DE GUICHE [shrugging his shoulders].
Good! let me pass!

CYRANO [intercepting him].
Where am I? Tell the truth!
Fear not to tell! Oh, spare me not! Where? where?
Have I fallen like a shooting star?

DE GUICHE.
Morbleu!

CYRANO.
The fall was lightning-quick! no time to choose
Where I should fall--I know not where it be!
Oh, tell me! Is it on a moon or earth,
that my posterior weight has landed me?

DE GUICHE.
I tell you, Sir. . .

CYRANO [with a screech of terror, which makes De Guiche
start back].
No? Can it be? I'm on
A planet where men have black faces?

DE GUICHE [putting a hand to his face].
What?

CYRANO [feigning great alarm].
Am I in Africa? A native you?

DE GUICHE [who has remembered his mask].
This mask of mine. . .

CYRANO [pretending to be reassured].
In Venice? ha!--or Rome?

DE GUICHE [trying to pass].
A lady waits. . .

CYRANO [quite reassured].
Oh-ho! I am in Paris!

DE GUICHE [smiling in spite of himself].
The fool is comical!

CYRANO.
You laugh?

DE GUICHE.
I laugh,
But would get by!

CYRANO [beaming with joy].
I have shot back to Paris!
[Quite at ease, laughing, dusting himself, bowing]
Come--pardon me--by the last water-spout,
Covered with ether,--accident of travel!
My eyes still full of star-dust, and my spurs
Encumbered by the planets' filaments!
[Picking something off his sleeve]
Ha! on my doublet?--ah, a comet's hair!. . .

[He puffs as if to blow it away.]

DE GUICHE [beside himself].
Sir!. . .

CYRANO [just as he is about to pass, holds out his leg as if to show
him something and stops him].

In my leg--the calf--there is a tooth
Of the Great Bear, and, passing Neptune close,
I would avoid his trident's point, and fell,
Thus sitting, plump, right in the Scales! My weight
Is marked, still registered, up there in heaven!
[Hurriedly preventing De Guiche from passing, and detaining him by
the button of his doublet]
I swear to you that if you squeezed my nose
It would spout milk!

DE GUICHE.
Milk?

CYRANO.
From the Milky Way!

DE GUICHE.
Oh, go to hell!

CYRANO [crossing his arms].
I fall, Sir, out of heaven!
Now, would you credit it, that as I fell
I saw that Sirius wears a nightcap? True!
[Confidentially]
The other Bear is still too small to bite.
[Laughing]
I went through the Lyre, but I snapped a cord;
[Grandiloquent]
I mean to write the whole thing in a book;
The small gold stars, that, wrapped up in my cloak,
I carried safe away at no small risks,
Will serve for asterisks i' the printed page!

DE GUICHE.
Come, make an end! I want. . .

CYRANO.
Oh-ho! You are sly!

DE GUICHE.
Sir!

CYRANO.
You would worm all out of me!--the way
The moon is made, and if men breathe and live
In its rotund cucurbita?

DE GUICHE [angrily].
No, no!
I want. . .

CYRANO.
Ha, ha!--to know how I got up?
Hark, it was by a method all my own.

DE GUICHE [wearied].
He's mad!

CYRANO [contemptuously].
No! not for me the stupid eagle
Of Regiomontanus, nor the timid
Pigeon of Archytas--neither of those!

DE GUICHE.
Ay, 'tis a fool! But 'tis a learned fool!

CYRANO.
No imitator I of other men!
[De Guiche has succeeded in getting by, and goes toward Roxane's
door. Cyrano follows him, ready to stop him by force.]
Six novel methods, all, this brain invented!

DE GUICHE [turning round].
Six?

CYRANO [volubly].
First, with body naked as your hand,
Festooned about with crystal flacons, full
O' th' tears the early morning dew distils;
My body to the sun's fierce rays exposed
To let it suck me up, as 't sucks the dew!

DE GUICHE [surprised, making one step toward Cyrano].
Ah! that makes one!

CYRANO [stepping back, and enticing him further away].
And then, the second way,
To generate wind--for my impetus--
To rarefy air, in a cedar case,
By mirrors placed icosahedron-wise.

DE GUICHE [making another step].
Two!

CYRANO [still stepping backward].
Or--for I have some mechanic skill--
To make a grasshopper, with springs of steel,
And launch myself by quick succeeding fires
Saltpeter-fed to the stars' pastures blue!

DE GUICHE [unconsciously following him and counting on his
fingers].
Three!

CYRANO.
Or (since fumes have property to mount)--
To charge a globe with fumes, sufficiently
To carry me aloft!

DE GUICHE [same play, more and more astonished].
Well, that makes four!

CYRANO.
Or smear myself with marrow from a bull,
Since, at the lowest point of Zodiac,
Phoebus well loves to suck that marrow up!

DE GUICHE [amazed].
Five!

CYRANO [who, while speaking, had drawn him to the other side of
the square near a bench].
Sitting on an iron platform--thence
To throw a magnet in the air. This is
A method well conceived--the magnet flown,
Infallibly the iron will pursue:
Then quick! relaunch your magnet, and you thus
Can mount and mount unmeasured distances!

DE GUICHE.
Here are six excellent expedients!
Which of the six chose you?

CYRANO.
Why, none!--a seventh!

DE GUICHE.
Astonishing! What was it?

CYRANO.
I'll recount.

DE GUICHE.
This wild eccentric becomes interesting!

CYRANO [making a noise like the waves, with weird gestures].
Houuh! Houuh!

DE GUICHE.
Well.

CYRANO.
You have guessed?

DE GUICHE.
Not I!

CYRANO.
The tide!
I' th' witching hour when the moon woos the wave,
I laid me, fresh from a sea-bath, on the shore--
And, failing not to put head foremost--for
The hair holds the sea-water in its mesh--
I rose in air, straight! straight! like angel's flight,
And mounted, mounted, gently, effortless,. . .
When lo! a sudden shock! Then. . .

DE GUICHE [overcome by curiosity, sitting down on the bench].
Then?

CYRANO.
Oh! then. . .
[Suddenly returning to his natural voice]
The quarter's gone--I'll hinder you no more:
The marriage-vows are made.

DE GUICHE [springing up].
What? Am I mad?
That voice?
[The house-door opens. Lackeys appear carrying lighted candelabra.
Light. Cyrano gracefully uncovers.]

That nose--Cyrano?

CYRANO [bowing].
Cyrano.
While we were chatting, they have plighted troth.

DE GUICHE.
Who?
[He turns round. Tableau. Behind the lackeys appear Roxane and
Christian, holding each other by the hand. The friar follows them,
smiling. Ragueneau also holds a candlestick. The duenna closes the
rear, bewildered, having made a hasty toilet.]
Heavens!

Act III. Scene XII.

[The same. Roxane, Christian, the friar, Ragueneau, lackeys, the
duenna.]

DE GUICHE [to Roxane].
You?
[Recognizing Christian, in amazement]
He?
[Bowing, with admiration, to Roxane]
Cunningly contrived!
[To Cyrano]
My compliments--Sir Apparatus-maker!
Your story would arrest at Peter's gate
Saints eager for their Paradise! Note well
The details. 'Faith! They'd make a stirring book!

CYRANO [bowing]
I shall not fail to follow your advice.

THE FRIAR [showing with satisfaction the two lovers to De Guiche].
A handsome couple, son, made one by you!

DE GUICHE [with a freezing look].
Ay!
[To Roxane]
Bid your bridegroom, Madame, fond farewell.

ROXANE.
Why so?

DE GUICHE [to Christian].
Even now the regiment departs.
Join it!

ROXANE.
It goes to battle?

DE GUICHE.
Without doubt.

ROXANE.
But the Cadets go not?

DE GUICHE.
Oh ay! they go.
[Drawing out the paper he had put in his pocket]
Here is the order.
[To Christian]
Baron, bear it, quick!

ROXANE [throwing herself in Christian's arms].
Christian!

DE GUICHE [sneeringly to Cyrano].
The wedding-night is far, methinks!

CYRANO [aside].
He thinks to give me pain of death by this!

CHRISTIAN [to Roxane].
Oh! once again! Your lips!

CYRANO.
Come, come, enough!

CHRISTIAN [still kissing Roxane].
--'Tis hard to leave her, you know not. . .

CYRANO [trying to draw him away].
I know.

       [Sound of drums beating a march in the distance.]

DE GUICHE.
The regiment starts!

ROXANE [To Cyrano, holding back Christian, whom Cyrano is drawing away].
Oh!--I trust him you!
Promise me that no risks shall put his life
In danger!

CYRANO.
I will try my best, but promise. . .
That I cannot!

ROXANE.
But swear he shall be prudent?

CYRANO.
Again, I'll do my best, but. . .

ROXANE.
In the siege
Let him not suffer!

CYRANO.
All that man can do,
I. . .

ROXANE.
That he shall be faithful!

CYRANO.
Doubtless, but. . .

ROXANE.
That he will write oft?

CYRANO [pausing].
That, I promise you!

[Curtain.]

ACT IV

The Cadets of Gascony.

Post occupied by company of Carbon de Castel-Jaloux at the siege of Arras.

In the background an embankment across the whole stage. Beyond, view of plain extending to the horizon. The country covered with intrenchments. The walls of Arras and the outlines of its roofs against the sky in the distance. Tents. Arms strewn about, drums, etc. Day is breaking with a faint glimmer of yellow sunrise in the east. Sentinels at different points. Watch-fires. The cadets of Gascony, wrapped in their mantles, are sleeping. Carbon de Castel-Jaloux and Le Bret are keeping watch. They are very pale and thin. Christian sleeps among the others in his cloak in the foreground, his face illuminated by the fire. Silence.

Act IV. Scene I.

[Christian, Carbon de Castel-Jaloux, Le Bret, the cadets, then Cyrano.]

LE BRET.

'Tis terrible.

CARBON.
Not a morsel left.

LE BRET.
Mordioux!

CARBON [making a sign that he should speak lower].
Curse under your breath. You will awake them.
[To the cadets]
Hush! Sleep on.
[To Le Bret]
He who sleeps, dines!

LE BRET.
But that is sorry comfort for the sleepless!. . .
What starvation!

[Firing is heard in the distance.]

CARBON.
Oh, plague take their firing! 'Twill wake my sons.
[To the cadets, who lift up their heads]
Sleep on!

[Firing is again heard, nearer this time.]

A CADET [moving].
The devil!. . .Again.

CARBON.
'Tis nothing! 'Tis Cyrano coming back!

[Those who have lifted up their heads prepare to sleep again.]

A SENTINEL [from without].
Ventrebieu! Who goes there?

THE VOICE Of CYRANO.
Bergerac.

The SENTINEL [who is on the redoubt].
Ventrebieu! Who goes there?

CYRANO [appearing at the top].
Bergerac, idiot!

[He comes down; Le Bret advances anxiously to meet him.]

LE BRET.
Heavens!

CYRANO [making signs that he should not awake the others].
Hush!

LE BRET.
Wounded?

CYRANO.
Oh! you know it has become their custom to shoot at me every morning and to miss me.

LE BRET.
This passes all! To take letters at each day's dawn. To risk. . .

CYRANO [stopping before Christian].
I promised he should write often.
[He looks at him.]
He sleeps. How pale he is! But how handsome still, despite his sufferings.
If his poor little lady-love knew that he is dying of hunger. . .

LE BRET.
Get you quick to bed.

CYRANO.
Nay, never scold, Le Bret. I ran but little risk. I have found me a spot to pass the Spanish lines, where each night they lie drunk.

LE BRET.
You should try to bring us back provision.

CYRANO.
A man must carry no weight who would get by there! But there will be surprise for us this night. The French will eat or die. . .if I mistake not!

LE BRET.
Oh!. . .tell me!. . .

CYRANO.
Nay, not yet. I am not certain. . .You will see!

CARBON.
It is disgraceful that we should starve while we're besieging!

LE BRET.
Alas, how full of complication is this siege of Arras! To think that while we are besieging, we should ourselves be caught in a trap and besieged by the Cardinal Infante of Spain.

CYRANO.
It were well done if he should be besieged in his turn.

LE BRET.
I am in earnest.

CYRANO.
Oh! indeed!

LE BRET.
To think you risk a life so precious. . .for the sake of a letter. . .Thank-
less one.
[Seeing him turning to enter the tent]
Where are you going?

CYRANO.
I am going to write another.

[He enters the tent and disappears.]

Act IV. Scene II.

[The same, all but Cyrano. The day is breaking in a rosy light. The
town of Arras is golden in the horizon. The report of cannon is heard
in the distance, followed immediately by the beating of drums far away
to the left. Other drums are heard much nearer. Sounds of stirring in
the camp. Voices of officers in the distance.]

CARBON [sighing].
The reveille!
[The cadets move and stretch themselves.]
Nourishing sleep! Thou art at an end!. . .I know well what will be their
first cry!

A CADET [sitting up].
I am so hungry!

ANOTHER.
I am dying of hunger.

TOGETHER.
Oh!

CARBON.
Up with you!

THIRD CADET.
--Cannot move a limb.

FOURTH CADET.
Nor can I.

THE FIRST [looking at himself in a bit of armor].
My tongue is yellow. The air at this season of the year is hard to digest.

ANOTHER.
My coronet for a bit of Chester!

ANOTHER.
If none can furnish to my gaster wherewith to make a pint of chyle, I shall retire to my tent--like Achilles!

ANOTHER.
Oh! something! were it but a crust!

CARBON [going to the tent and calling softly].
Cyrano!

ALL THE CADETS.
We are dying!

CARBON [continuing to speak under his breath at the opening of the tent].
Come to my aid, you, who have the art of quick retort and gay jest. Come, hearten them up.

SECOND CADET [rushing toward another who is munching something].
What are you crunching there?

FIRST CADET.

Cannon-wads soaked in axle-grease! 'Tis poor hunting round about Arras!

A CADET [entering].
I have been after game.

ANOTHER [following him].
And I after fish.

ALL [rushing to the two newcomers].
Well! what have you brought?--a pheasant?--a carp?--Come, show us quick!

THE ANGLER.
A gudgeon!

THE SPORTSMAN.
A sparrow!

ALL TOGETHER [beside themselves].
'Tis more than can be borne! We will mutiny!

CARBON.
Cyrano! Come to my help.

[The daylight has now come.]

Act IV. Scene III.

[The SAME. Cyrano.]

CYRANO [appearing from the tent, very calm, with a pen stuck behind his ear and a book in his hand].
What is wrong?
[Silence. To the first cadet]
Why drag you your legs so sorrowfully?

THE CADET.
I have something in my heels which weighs them down.

CYRANO.
And what may that be?

THE CADET.
My stomach!

CYRANO.
So have I, 'faith!

THE CADET.
It must be in your way?

CYRANO.
Nay, I am all the taller.

A THIRD.
My stomach's hollow.

CYRANO.
'Faith, 'twill make a fine drum to sound the assault.

ANOTHER.
I have a ringing in my ears.

CYRANO.
No, no, 'tis false; a hungry stomach has no ears.

ANOTHER.
Oh, to eat something--something oily!

CYRANO [pulling off the cadet's helmet and holding it out to him].
Behold your salad!

ANOTHER.
What, in God's name, can we devour?

CYRANO [throwing him the book which he is carrying].
The 'Iliad'.

ANOTHER.
The first minister in Paris has his four meals a day!

CYRANO.
'Twere courteous an he sent you a few partridges!

THE SAME.
And why not? with wine, too!

CYRANO.
A little Burgundy. Richelieu, s'il vous plait!

THE SAME.
He could send it by one of his friars.

CYRANO.
Ay! by His Eminence Joseph himself.

ANOTHER.
I am as ravenous as an ogre!

CYRANO.
Eat your patience, then.

THE FIRST CADET [shrugging his shoulders].
Always your pointed word!

CYRANO.
Ay, pointed words!

I would fain die thus, some soft summer eve,
Making a pointed word for a good cause.
--To make a soldier's end by soldier's sword,
Wielded by some brave adversary--die
On blood-stained turf, not on a fever-bed,
A point upon my lips, a point within my heart.

CRIES FROM ALL.
I'm hungry!

CYRANO [crossing his arms].
All your thoughts of meat and drink!
Bertrand the fifer!--you were shepherd once,--
Draw from its double leathern case your fife,
Play to these greedy, guzzling soldiers. Play
Old country airs with plaintive rhythm recurring,
Where lurk sweet echoes of the dear home-voices,
Each note of which calls like a little sister,
Those airs slow, slow ascending, as the smoke-wreaths
Rise from the hearthstones of our native hamlets,
Their music strikes the ear like Gascon patois!. . .
[The old man seats himself, and gets his flute ready.]
Your flute was now a warrior in durance;
But on its stem your fingers are a-dancing
A bird-like minuet! O flute! Remember
That flutes were made of reeds first, not laburnum;
Make us a music pastoral days recalling--
The soul-time of your youth, in country pastures!. . .
[The old man begins to play the airs of Languedoc.]
Hark to the music, Gascons!. . .'Tis no longer
The piercing fife of camp--but 'neath his fingers
The flute of the woods! No more the call to combat,
'Tis now the love-song of the wandering goat-herds!. . .
Hark!. . .'tis the valley, the wet landes, the forest,
The sunburnt shepherd-boy with scarlet beret,

The dusk of evening on the Dordogne river,--
'Tis Gascony! Hark, Gascons, to the music!

[The cadets sit with bowed heads; their eyes have a far-off look as if
dreaming, and they surreptitiously wipe away their tears with their
cuffs and the corner of their cloaks.]

CARBON [to Cyrano in a whisper].
But you make them weep!

CYRANO.
Ay, for homesickness. A nobler pain than hunger,--'tis of the soul, not
of the body! I am well pleased to see their pain change its viscera.
Heart-ache is better than stomach-ache.

CARBON.
But you weaken their courage by playing thus on their heart-strings!

CYRANO [making a sign to a drummer to approach].
Not I. The hero that sleeps in Gascon blood is ever ready to awake
in them.
'Twould suffice. . .

[He makes a signal; the drum beats.]

ALL THE CADETS [stand up and rush to take arms].
What? What is it?

CYRANO [smiling].
You see! One roll of the drum is enough! Good-by dreams, regrets,
native land, love. . .All that the pipe called forth the drum has chased
away!

A CADET [looking toward the back of the stage].
Ho! here comes Monsieur de Guiche.

ALL THE CADETS [muttering].
Ugh!. . .Ugh!. . .

CYRANO [smiling].
A flattering welcome!

A CADET.
We are sick to death of him!

ANOTHER CADET.
--With his lace collar over his armor, playing the fine gentleman!

ANOTHER.
As if one wore linen over steel!

THE FIRST.
It were good for a bandage had he boils on his neck.

THE SECOND.
Another plotting courtier!

ANOTHER CADET.
His uncle's own nephew!

CARBON.
For all that--a Gascon.

THE FIRST.
Ay, false Gascon!. . .trust him not. . .
Gascons should ever be crack-brained. . .
Naught more dangerous than a rational Gascon.

LE BRET.
How pale he is!

ANOTHER.

Oh! he is hungry, just like us poor devils; but under his cuirass, with its fine gilt nails, his stomach-ache glitters brave in the sun.

CYRANO [hurriedly].
Let us not seem to suffer either! Out with your cards, pipes, and dice...
[All begin spreading out the games on the drums, the stools, the ground, and on their cloaks, and light long pipes.]
And I shall read Descartes.

[He walks up and down, reading a little book which he has drawn from his pocket. Tableau. Enter De Guiche. All appear absorbed and happy. He is very pale. He goes up to Carbon.]

Act IV. Scene IV.

[The same. De Guiche.]

DE GUICHE [to Carbon].
Good-day!
[They examine each other. Aside, with satisfaction]
He's green.

CARBON [aside].
He has nothing left but eyes.

DE GUICHE [looking at the cadets].
Here are the rebels! Ay, Sirs, on all sides
I hear that in your ranks you scoff at me;
That the Cadets, these loutish, mountain-bred,
Poor country squires, and barons of Perigord,
Scarce find for me--their Colonel--a disdain
Sufficient! call me plotter, wily courtier!
It does not please their mightiness to see
A point-lace collar on my steel cuirass,--
And they enrage, because a man, in sooth,

May be no ragged-robin, yet a Gascon!
[Silence. All smoke and play]
Shall I command your Captain punish you?
No.

CARBON.
I am free, moreover,--will not punish--

DE GUICHE.
Ah!

CARBON.
I have paid my company--'tis mine.
I bow but to headquarters.

DE GUICHE.
So?--in faith!
That will suffice.
[Addressing himself to the cadets]
I can despise your taunts
'Tis well known how I bear me in the war;
At Bapaume, yesterday, they saw the rage
With which I beat back the Count of Bucquoi;
Assembling my own men, I fell on his,
And charged three separate times!

CYRANO [without lifting his eyes from his book].
And your white scarf?

DE GUICHE [surprised and gratified].
You know that detail?. . .Troth! It happened thus:
While caracoling to recall the troops
For the third charge, a band of fugitives
Bore me with them, close by the hostile ranks:
I was in peril--capture, sudden death!--

When I thought of the good expedient
To loosen and let fall the scarf which told
My military rank; thus I contrived
--Without attention waked--to leave the foes,
And suddenly returning, reinforced
With my own men, to scatter them! And now,
--What say you, Sir?

[The cadets pretend not to be listening, but the cards and the dice-
boxes remain suspended in their hands, the smoke of their pipes in
their cheeks. They wait.]

CYRANO.
I say, that Henri Quatre
Had not, by any dangerous odds, been forced
To strip himself of his white helmet plume.

[Silent delight. The cards fall, the dice rattle. The smoke is puffed.]

DE GUICHE.
The ruse succeeded, though!

[Same suspension of play, etc.]

CYRANO.
Oh, may be! But
One does not lightly abdicate the honor
To serve as target to the enemy
[Cards, dice, fall again, and the cadets smoke with evident delight.]
Had I been present when your scarf fell low,
--Our courage, Sir, is of a different sort--
I would have picked it up and put it on.

DE GUICHE.
Oh, ay! Another Gascon boast!

CYRANO.
A boast?
Lend it to me. I pledge myself, to-night,
--With it across my breast,--to lead th' assault.

DE GUICHE.
Another Gascon vaunt! You know the scarf
Lies with the enemy, upon the brink
Of the stream,. . .the place is riddled now with shot,--
No one can fetch it hither!

CYRANO [drawing the scarf from his pocket, and holding it out
to him]
Here it is.

[Silence. The cadets stifle their laughter in their cards and dice-boxes.
De Guiche turns and looks at them; they instantly become grave, and
set to play. One of them whistles indifferently the air just played by
the fifer.]

DE GUICHE [taking the scarf].
I thank you. It will now enable me
To make a signal,--that I had forborne
To make--till now.

[He goes to the rampart, climbs it, and waves the scarf thrice.]

ALL.
What's that?

THE SENTINEL [from the top of the rampart].
See you yon man
Down there, who runs?. . .

DE GUICHE [descending].
'Tis a false Spanish spy

Who is extremely useful to my ends.
The news he carries to the enemy
Are those I prompt him with--so, in a word,
We have an influence on their decisions!

CYRANO.
Scoundrel!

DE GUICHE [carelessly knotting on his scarf].
'Tis opportune. What were we saying?
Ah! I have news for you. Last evening
--To victual us--the Marshal did attempt
A final effort:--secretly he went
To Dourlens, where the King's provisions be.
But--to return to camp more easily--
He took with him a goodly force of troops.
Those who attacked us now would have fine sport!
Half of the army's absent from the camp!

CARBON.
Ay, if the Spaniards knew, 'twere ill for us,
But they know nothing of it?

DE GUICHE.
Oh! they know.
They will attack us.

CARBON.
Ah!

DE GUICHE.
For my false spy
Came to warn me of their attack. He said,
'I can decide the point for their assault;
Where would you have it? I will tell them 'tis
The least defended--they'll attempt you there.'

I answered, 'Good. Go out of camp, but watch
My signal. Choose the point from whence it comes.'

CARBON [to cadets].
Make ready!

[All rise; sounds of swords and belts being buckled.]

DE GUICHE.
'Twill be in an hour.

FIRST CADET.
Good!. . .

[They all sit down again and take up their games.]

DE GUICHE [to Carbon].
Time must be gained. The Marshal will return.

CARBON.
How gain it?

DE GUICHE.
You will all be good enough
To let yourselves to be killed.

CYRANO.
Vengeance! oho!

DE GUICHE.
I do not say that, if I loved you well,
I had chosen you and yours,--but, as things stand,--
Your courage yielding to no corps the palm--
I serve my King, and serve my grudge as well.

CYRANO.

Permit that I express my gratitude. . .

DE GUICHE.
I know you love to fight against five score;
You will not now complain of paltry odds.

[He goes up with Carbon.]

CYRANO [to the cadets].
We shall add to the Gascon coat of arms,
With its six bars of blue and gold, one more--
The blood-red bar that was a-missing there!

[De Guiche speaks in a low voice with Carbon at the back. Orders are
given. Preparations go forward. Cyrano goes up to Christian, who
stands with crossed arms.]

CYRANO [putting his hand on Christian's shoulder].
Christian!

CHRISTIAN [shaking his head].
Roxane!

CYRANO.
Alas!

CHRISTIAN.
At least, I'd send
My heart's farewell to her in a fair letter!. . .

CYRANO.
I had suspicion it would be to-day,
[He draws a letter out of his doublet.]
And had already writ. . .

CHRISTIAN.

Show!

CYRANO.
Will you. . .?

CHRISTIAN [taking the letter].
Ay!
[He opens and reads it.]
Hold!

CYRANO.
What?

CHRISTIAN.
This little spot!

CYRANO [taking the letter, with an innocent look].
A spot?

CHRISTIAN.
A tear!

CYRANO.
Poets, at last,--by dint of counterfeiting--
Take counterfeit for true--that is the charm!
This farewell letter,--it was passing sad,
I wept myself in writing it!

CHRISTIAN.
Wept? why?

CYRANO.
Oh!. . .death itself is hardly terrible,. . .
--But, ne'er to see her more! That is death's sting!
--For. . .I shall never. . .
[Christian looks at him.]

We shall. . .
[Quickly]
I mean, you. . .

CHRISTIAN [snatching the letter from him].
Give me that letter!

[A rumor, far off in the camp.]

VOICE Of SENTINEL.
Who goes there? Halloo!

[Shots--voices--carriage-bells.]

CARBON.
What is it?

A SENTINEL [on the rampart].
'Tis a carriage!

[All rush to see.]

CRIES.
In the camp?
It enters!--It comes from the enemy!
--Fire!--No!--The coachman cries!--What does he say?
--'On the King's service!'

[Everyone is on the rampart, staring. The bells come nearer.]

DE GUICHE.
The King's service? How?

[All descend and draw up in line.]

CARBON.

Uncover, all!

DE GUICHE.
The King's! Draw up in line!
Let him describe his curve as it befits!

[The carriage enters at full speed covered with dust and mud. The curtains are drawn close. Two lackeys behind. It is pulled up suddenly.]

CARBON.
Beat a salute!

[A roll of drums. The cadets uncover.]

DE GUICHE.
Lower the carriage-steps!

[Two cadets rush forward. The door opens.]

ROXANE [jumping down from the carriage].
Good-day!

[All are bowing to the ground, but at the sound of a woman's voice every head is instantly raised.]

Act IV. Scene V.

[The same. Roxane.]

DE GUICHE.
On the King's service! You?

ROXANE.
Ay,--King Love's! What other king?

CYRANO.

Great God!

CHRISTIAN [rushing forward].
Why have you come?

ROXANE.
This siege--'tis too long!

CHRISTIAN.
But why?. . .

ROXANE.
I will tell you all!

CYRANO [who, at the sound of her voice, has stood still, rooted to
the ground, afraid to raise his eyes].
My God! dare I look at her?

DE GUICHE.
You cannot remain here!

ROXANE [merrily].
But I say yes! Who will push a drum hither for me?
[She seats herself on the drum they roll forward.]
So! I thank you.
[She laughs.]
My carriage was fired at
[proudly]
by the patrol! Look! would you not think 'twas made of a pumpkin, like
Cinderella's chariot in the tale,--and the footmen out of rats?
[Sending a kiss with her lips to Christian]
Good-morrow!
[Examining them all]
You look not merry, any of you! Ah! know you that 'tis a long road to
get to Arras?
[Seeing Cyrano]

Cousin, delighted!

CYRANO [coming up to her].
But how, in Heaven's name?. . .

ROXANE.
How found I the way to the army? It was simple enough, for I had but to pass on and on, as far as I saw the country laid waste. Ah, what horrors were there! Had I not seen, then I could never have believed it! Well, gentlemen, if such be the service of your King, I would fainer serve mine!

CYRANO.
But 'tis sheer madness! Where in the fiend's name did you get through?

ROXANE.
Where? Through the Spanish lines.

FIRST CADET.
--For subtle craft, give me a woman!

DE GUICHE.
But how did you pass through their lines?

LE BRET.
Faith! that must have been a hard matter!. . .

ROXANE.
None too hard. I but drove quietly forward in my carriage, and when some hidalgo of haughty mien would have stayed me, lo! I showed at the window my sweetest smile, and these Senors being (with no disrespect to you) the most gallant gentlemen in the world,--I passed on!

CARBON.
True, that smile is a passport! But you must have been asked frequently to give an account of where you were going, Madame?

ROXANE.
Yes, frequently. Then I would answer, 'I go to see my lover.' At that
word the very fiercest Spaniard of them all would gravely shut the
carriage-door, and, with a gesture that a king might envy, make signal
to his men to lower the muskets leveled at me;--then, with melancholy
but withal very graceful dignity--his beaver held to the wind that the
plumes might flutter bravely, he would bow low, saying to me, 'Pass on,
Senorita!'

CHRISTIAN.
But, Roxane. . .

ROXANE.
Forgive me that I said, 'my lover!' But bethink you, had I said 'my
husband,' not one of them had let me pass!

CHRISTIAN.
But. . .

ROXANE.
What ails you?

DE GUICHE.
You must leave this place!

ROXANE.
I?

CYRANO.
And that instantly!

LE BRET.
No time to lose.

CHRISTIAN.
Indeed, you must.

ROXANE.
But wherefore must I?

CHRISTIAN [embarrassed].
'Tis that. . .

CYRANO [the same].
--In three quarters of an hour. . .

DE GUICHE [the same].
--Or for. . .

CARBON [the same].
It were best. . .

LE BRET [the same].
You might. . .

ROXANE.
You are going to fight?--I stay here.

ALL.
No, no!

ROXANE.
He is my husband!
[She throws herself into Christian's arms.]
They shall kill us both together!

CHRISTIAN.
Why do you look at me thus?

ROXANE.
I will tell you why!

DE GUICHE [in despair].

'Tis a post of mortal danger!

ROXANE [turning round].
Mortal danger!

CYRANO.
Proof enough, that he has put us here!

ROXANE [to De Guiche].
So, Sir, you would have made a widow of me?

DE GUICHE.
Nay, on my oath. . .

ROXANE.
I will not go! I am reckless now, and I shall not stir from here!--
Besides, 'tis amusing!

CYRANO.
Oh-ho! So our precieuse is a heroine!

ROXANE.
Monsieur de Bergerac, I am your cousin.

A CADET.
We will defend you well!

ROXANE [more and more excited].
I have no fear of that, my friends!

ANOTHER [in ecstasy].
The whole camp smells sweet of orris-root!

ROXANE.
And, by good luck, I have chosen a hat that will suit well with the
battlefield!

[Looking at De Guiche]
But were it not wisest that the Count retire?
They may begin the attack.

DE GUICHE.
That is not to be brooked! I go to inspect the cannon, and shall return.
You have still time--think better of it!

ROXANE.
Never!

[De Guiche goes out.]

Act IV. Scene VI.

[The same, all but De Guiche.]

CHRISTIAN [entreatingly].
Roxane!

ROXANE.
No!

FIRST CADET [to the others].
She stays!

ALL [hurrying, hustling each other, tidying themselves].
A comb!--Soap!--My uniform is torn!--A needle!--A ribbon!--Lend your
mirror!--My cuffs!--Your curling-iron!--A razor!. . .

ROXANE [to Cyrano, who still pleads with her].
No! Naught shall make me stir from this spot!

CARBON [who, like the others, has been buckling, dusting, brushing
his hat, settling his plume, and drawing on his cuffs, advances to
Roxane, and ceremoniously].

It is perchance more seemly, since things are thus, that I present to you some of these gentlemen who are about to have the honor of dying before your eyes.
[Roxane bows, and stands leaning on Christian's arm, while Carbon introduces the cadets to her.]
Baron de Peyrescous de Colignac!

THE CADET [with a low reverence].
Madame. . .

CARBON [continuing].
Baron de Casterac de Cahuzac,—Vidame de Malgouyre Estressac Lesbas d'Escarabiot, Chevalier d'Antignac-Juzet, Baron Hillot de Blagnac-Salechan de Castel Crabioules. . .

ROXANE.
But how many names have you each?

BARON HILLOT.
Scores!

CARBON [to Roxane].
Pray, upon the hand that holds your kerchief.

ROXANE [opens her hand, and the handkerchief falls].
Why?

[The whole company start forward to pick it up.]

CARBON [quickly raising it].
My company had no flag. But now, by my faith, they will have the fairest in all the camp!

ROXANE [smiling].
'Tis somewhat small.

CARBON [tying the handkerchief on the staff of his lance].
But--'tis of lace!

A CADET [to the rest].
I could die happy, having seen so sweet a face, if I had something in my
stomach--were it but a nut!

CARBON [who has overheard, indignantly].
Shame on you! What, talk of eating when a lovely woman!. . .

ROXANE.
But your camp air is keen; I myself am famished. Pasties, cold fricas-
see, old wines--there is my bill of fare? Pray bring it all here.

[Consternation.]

A CADET.
All that?

ANOTHER.
But where on earth find it?

ROXANE [quietly].
In my carriage.

ALL.
How?

ROXANE.
Now serve up--carve! Look a little closer at my coachman, gentlemen,
and you will recognize a man most welcome. All the sauces can be sent
to table hot, if we will!

THE CADETS [rushing pellmell to the carriage].
'Tis Ragueneau!
[Acclamations]

Oh, oh!

ROXANE [looking after them].
Poor fellows!

CYRANO [kissing her hand].
Kind fairy!

RAGUENEAU [standing on the box like a quack doctor at a fair].
Gentlemen!. . .

[General delight.]

THE CADETS.
Bravo! bravo!

RAGUENEAU.
. . .The Spaniards, gazing on a lady so dainty fair, overlooked the fare so dainty!. . .

[Applause.]

CYRANO [in a whisper to Christian].
Hark, Christian!

RAGUENEAU.
. . .And, occupied with gallantry, perceived not--
[His draws a plate from under the seat, and holds it up.]
--The galantine!. . .

[Applause. The galantine passes from hand to hand.]

CYRANO [still whispering to Christian].
Prythee, one word!

RAGUENEAU.

And Venus so attracted their eyes that Diana could secretly pass
by with--
[He holds up a shoulder of mutton.]
--her fawn!

[Enthusiasm. Twenty hands are held out to seize the shoulder of
mutton.]

CYRANO [in a low whisper to Christian].
I must speak to you!

ROXANE [to the cadets, who come down, their arms laden
with food].
Put it all on the ground!

[She lays all out on the grass, aided by the two imperturbable lackeys
who were behind the carriage.]

ROXANE [to Christian, just as Cyrano is drawing him apart].
Come, make yourself of use!

[Christian comes to help her. Cyrano's uneasiness increases.]

RAGUENEAU.
Truffled peacock!

FIRST CADET [radiant, coming down, cutting a big slice
of ham].
By the mass! We shall not brave the last hazard without having had a
gullet-full!--
[quickly correcting himself on seeing Roxane]
--Pardon! A Balthazar feast!

RAGUENEAU [throwing down the carriage cushions].
The cushions are stuffed with ortolans!

[Hubbub. They tear open and turn out the contents of the cushions.
Bursts of laughter--merriment.]

THIRD CADET.
Ah! Viedaze!

RAGUENEAU [throwing down to the cadets bottles of red wine].
Flasks of rubies!--
(and white wine)
--Flasks of topaz!

ROXANE [throwing a folded tablecloth at Cyrano's head].
Unfold me that napkin!--Come, come! be nimble!

RAGUENEAU [waving a lantern].
Each of the carriage-lamps is a little larder!

CYRANO [in a low voice to Christian, as they arrange the cloth
together].
I must speak with you ere you speak to her.

RAGUENEAU.
My whip-handle is an Arles sausage!

ROXANE [pouring out wine, helping].
Since we are to die, let the rest of the army shift for itself. All for the
Gascons! And mark! if De Guiche comes, let no one invite him!
[Going from one to the other]
There! there! You have time enough! Do not eat too fast!--Drink a
little.-
-Why are you crying?

FIRST CADET.
It is all so good!. . .

ROXANE.

Tut!--Red or white?--Some bread for Monsieur de Carbon!--a knife!
Pass your plate!--a little of the crust? Some more? Let me help you!--
Some champagne?-
-A wing?

CYRANO [who follows her, his arms laden with dishes, helping her to
wait on everybody].
How I worship her!

ROXANE [going up to Christian].
What will you?

CHRISTIAN.
Nothing.

ROXANE.
Nay, nay, take this biscuit, steeped in muscat; come!. . .but two drops!

CHRISTIAN [trying to detain her].
Oh! tell me why you came?

ROXANE.
Wait; my first duty is to these poor fellows.--Hush! In a few minutes. .
.

LE BRET [who had gone up to pass a loaf on the end of a lance to the
sentry on the rampart].
De Guiche!

CYRANO.
Quick! hide flasks, plates, pie-dishes, game-baskets! Hurry!--Let us all
look unconscious!
[To Ragueneau]
Up on your seat!--Is everything covered up?

[In an instant all has been pushed into the tents, or hidden under doublets, cloaks, and beavers. De Guiche enters hurriedly--stops suddenly, sniffing the air. Silence.]

Act IV. Scene VII.

[The same. De Guiche.]

DE GUICHE.
It smells good here.

A CADET [humming].
Lo! Lo-lo!

DE GUICHE [looking at him].
What is the matter?--You are very red.

THE CADET.
The matter?--Nothing!--'Tis my blood--boiling at the thought of the coming battle!

ANOTHER.
Poum, poum--poum. . .

DE GUICHE [turning round].
What's that?

THE CADET [slightly drunk].
Nothing!. . .'Tis a song!--a little. . .

DE GUICHE.
You are merry, my friend!

THE CADET.
The approach of danger is intoxicating!

DE GUICHE [calling Carbon de Castel-Jaloux, to give him an order].

Captain! I. . .
[He stops short on seeing him.]
Plague take me! but you look bravely, too!

CARBON [crimson in the face, hiding a bottle behind his back, with
an evasive movement].
Oh!. . .

DE GUICHE.
I have one cannon left, and have had it carried there--
[He points behind the scenes.]
--in that corner. . . Your men can use it in case of need.

A CADET [reeling slightly].
Charming attention!

ANOTHER [with a gracious smile].
Kind solicitude!

DE GUICHE.
How? they are all gone crazy?
[Drily]
As you are not used to cannon, beware of the recoil.

FIRST CADET.
Pooh!

DE GUICHE [furious, going up to him].
But. . .

THE CADET.
Gascon cannons never recoil!

DE GUICHE [taking him by the arm and shaking him].
You are tipsy!--but what with?

THE CADET [grandiloquently].
--With the smell of powder!

DE GUICHE [shrugging his shoulders and pushing him away, then going quickly to Roxane].
Briefly, Madame, what decision do you deign to take?

ROXANE.
I stay here.

DE GUICHE.
You must fly!

ROXANE.
No! I will stay.

DE GUICHE.
Since things are thus, give me a musket, one of you!

CARBON.
Wherefore?

DE GUICHE.
Because I too--mean to remain.

CYRANO.
At last! This is true valor, Sir!

FIRST CADET.
Then you are Gascon after all, spite of your lace collar?

ROXANE.
What is all this?

DE GUICHE.
I leave no woman in peril.

SECOND CADET [to the first].
Hark you! Think you not we might give him something to eat?

[All the viands reappear as if by magic.]

DE GUICHE [whose eyes sparkle].
Victuals!

THE THIRD CADET.
Yes, you'll see them coming from under every coat!

DE GUICHE [controlling himself, haughtily].
Do you think I will eat your leavings?

CYRANO [saluting him].
You make progress.

DE GUICHE [proudly, with a light touch of accent on the word
'breaking'].
I will fight without br-r-eaking my fast!

FIRST CADET [with wild delight].
Br-r-r-eaking! He has got the accent!

DE GUICHE [laughing].
I?

THE CADET.
'Tis a Gascon!

[All begin to dance.]

CARBON DE CASTEL-JALOUX [who had disappeared behind the
rampart, reappearing on the ridge].
I have drawn my pikemen up in line. They are a resolute troop.

[He points to a row of pikes, the tops of which are seen over
the ridge.]

DE GUICHE [bowing to Roxane].
Will you accept my hand, and accompany me while I review them?

[She takes it, and they go up toward the rampart. All uncover and
follow them.]

CHRISTIAN [going to Cyrano, eagerly].
Tell me quickly!

[As Roxane appears on the ridge, the tops of the lances disappear,
lowered for the salute, and a shout is raised. She bows.]

THE PIKEMEN [outside].
Vivat!

CHRISTIAN.
What is this secret?

CYRANO.
If Roxane should. . .

CHRISTIAN.
Should?. . .

CYRANO.
Speak of the letters?. . .

CHRISTIAN.
Yes, I know!. . .

CYRANO.
Do not spoil all by seeming surprised. . .

CHRISTIAN.
At what?

CYRANO.
I must explain to you!. . .Oh! 'tis no great matter--I but thought of it
to-day on seeing her. You have. . .

CHRISTIAN.
Tell quickly!

CYRANO.
You have. . .written to her oftener than you think. . .

CHRISTIAN.
How so?

CYRANO.
Thus, 'faith! I had taken it in hand to express your flame for you!. . .At
times I wrote without saying, 'I am writing!'

CHRISTIAN.
Ah!. . .

CYRANO.
'Tis simple enough!

CHRISTIAN.
But how did you contrive, since we have been cut off, thus. . .to?. . .

CYRANO.
. . .Oh! before dawn. . .I was able to get through. . .

CHRISTIAN [folding his arms].
That was simple, too? And how oft, pray you, have I written?. . .Twice
in the week?. . .Three times?. . .Four?. . .

CYRANO.
More often still.

CHRISTIAN.
What! Every day?

CYRANO.
Yes, every day,--twice.

CHRISTIAN [violently].
And that became so mad a joy for you, that you braved death. . .

CYRANO [seeing Roxane returning].
Hush! Not before her!

[He goes hurriedly into his tent.]

Act IV. Scene VIII.

[Roxane, Christian. In the distance cadets coming and going. Carbon
and De Guiche give orders.]

ROXANE [running up to Christian].
Ah, Christian, at last!. . .

CHRISTIAN [taking her hands].
Now tell me why--
Why, by these fearful paths so perilous--
Across these ranks of ribald soldiery,
You have come?

ROXANE.
Love, your letters brought me here!

CHRISTIAN.
What say you?

ROXANE.

'Tis your fault if I ran risks!
Your letters turned my head! Ah! all this month,
How many!--and the last one ever bettered
The one that went before!

CHRISTIAN.

What!--for a few
Inconsequent love-letters!

ROXANE.

Hold your peace!
Ah! you cannot conceive it! Ever since
That night, when, in a voice all new to me,
Under my window you revealed your soul--
Ah! ever since I have adored you! Now
Your letters all this whole month long!--meseemed
As if I heard that voice so tender, true,
Sheltering, close! Thy fault, I say! It drew me,
The voice o' th' night! Oh! wise Penelope
Would ne'er have stayed to broider on her hearthstone,
If her Ulysses could have writ such letters!
But would have cast away her silken bobbins,
And fled to join him, mad for love as Helen!

CHRISTIAN.

But. . .

ROXANE.

I read, read again--grew faint for love;
I was thine utterly. Each separate page
Was like a fluttering flower-petal, loosed
From your own soul, and wafted thus to mine.
Imprinted in each burning word was love
Sincere, all-powerful. . .

CHRISTIAN.
A love sincere!
Can that be felt, Roxane!

ROXANE.
Ay, that it can!

CHRISTIAN.
You come. . .?

ROXANE.
O, Christian, my true lord, I come--
(Were I to throw myself, here, at your knees,
You would raise me--but 'tis my soul I lay
At your feet--you can raise it nevermore!)
--I come to crave your pardon. (Ay, 'tis time
To sue for pardon, now that death may come!)
For the insult done to you when, frivolous,
At first I loved you only for your face!

CHRISTIAN [horror-stricken].
Roxane!

ROXANE.
And later, love--less frivolous--
Like a bird that spreads its wings, but can not fly--
Arrested by your beauty, by your soul
Drawn close--I loved for both at once!

CHRISTIAN.
And now?

ROXANE.
Ah! you yourself have triumphed o'er yourself,
And now, I love you only for your soul!

CHRISTIAN [stepping backward].
Roxane!

ROXANE.
Be happy. To be loved for beauty--
A poor disguise that time so soon wears threadbare--
Must be to noble souls--to souls aspiring--
A torture. Your dear thoughts have now effaced
That beauty that so won me at the outset.
Now I see clearer--and I no more see it!

CHRISTIAN.
Oh!. . .

ROXANE.
You are doubtful of such victory?

CHRISTIAN [pained].
Roxane!

ROXANE.
I see you cannot yet believe it.
Such love. . .?

CHRISTIAN.
I do not ask such love as that!
I would be loved more simply; for. . .

ROXANE.
For that
Which they have all in turns loved in thee?--
Shame!
Oh! be loved henceforth in a better way!

CHRISTIAN.
No! the first love was best!

ROXANE.
Ah! how you err!
'Tis now that I love best--love well! 'Tis that
Which is thy true self, see!--that I adore!
Were your brilliance dimmed. . .

CHRISTIAN.
Hush!

ROXANE.
I should love still!
Ay, if your beauty should to-day depart. . .

CHRISTIAN.
Say not so!

ROXANE.
Ay, I say it!

CHRISTIAN.
Ugly? How?

ROXANE.
Ugly! I swear I'd love you still!

CHRISTIAN.
My God!

ROXANE.
Are you content at last?

CHRISTIAN [in a choked voice].
Ay!. . .

ROXANE.
What is wrong?

CHRISTIAN [gently pushing her away].
Nothing. . .I have two words to say:--one second. . .

ROXANE.
But?. . .

CHRISTIAN [pointing to the cadets].
Those poor fellows, shortly doomed to death,--
My love deprives them of the sight of you:
Go,--speak to them--smile on them ere they die!

ROXANE [deeply affected].
Dear Christian!. . .

[She goes up to the cadets, who respectfully crowd round her.]

Act IV. Scene IX.

[Christian, Cyrano. At back Roxane talking to Carbon and some
cadets.]

CHRISTIAN [calling toward Cyrano's tent].
Cyrano!

CYRANO [reappearing, fully armed].
What? Why so pale?

CHRISTIAN.
She does not love me!

CYRANO.
What?

CHRISTIAN.
'Tis you she loves!

CYRANO.
No!

CHRISTIAN.
--For she loves me only for my soul!

CYRANO.
Truly?

CHRISTIAN.
Yes! Thus--you see, that soul is you,. . .
Therefore, 'tis you she loves!--And you--love her!

CYRANO.
I?

CHRISTIAN.
Oh, I know it!

CYRANO.
Ay, 'tis true!

CHRISTIAN.
You love
To madness!

CYRANO.
Ay! and worse!

CHRISTIAN.
Then tell her so!

CYRANO.
No!

CHRISTIAN.

And why not?

CYRANO.
Look at my face!--be answered!

CHRISTIAN.
She'd love me--were I ugly.

CYRANO.
Said she so?

CHRISTIAN.
Ay! in those words!

CYRANO.
I'm glad she told you that!
But pooh!--believe it not! I am well pleased
She thought to tell you. Take it not for truth.
Never grow ugly:--she'd reproach me then!

CHRISTIAN.
That I intend discovering!

CYRANO.
No! I beg!

CHRISTIAN.
Ay! she shall choose between us!--Tell her all!

CYRANO.
No! no! I will not have it! Spare me this!

CHRISTIAN.
Because my face is haply fair, shall I
Destroy your happiness? 'Twere too unjust!

CYRANO.

And I,--because by Nature's freak I have
The gift to say--all that perchance you feel.
Shall I be fatal to your happiness?

CHRISTIAN.

Tell all!

CYRANO.

It is ill done to tempt me thus!

CHRISTIAN.

Too long I've borne about within myself
A rival to myself--I'll make an end!

CYRANO.

Christian!

CHRISTIAN.

Or union, without witness--secret--
Clandestine--can be easily dissolved
If we survive.

CYRANO.

My God!--he still persists!

CHRISTIAN.

I will be loved myself--or not at all!
--I'll go see what they do--there, at the end
Of the post: speak to her, and then let her choose
One of us two!

CYRANO.

It will be you.

CHRISTIAN.

Pray God!
[He calls.]
Roxane!

CYRANO.
No! no!

ROXANE [coming up quickly].
What?

CHRISTIAN.
Cyrano has things
Important for your ear. . .

[She hastens to Cyrano. Christian goes out.]

Act IV. Scene X.

[Roxane, Cyrano. Then Le Bret, Carbon de Castel-Jaloux, the cadets,
Ragueneau, De Guiche, etc.]

ROXANE.
Important, how?

CYRANO [in despair. to Roxane].
He's gone! 'Tis naught!--Oh, you know how he sees
Importance in a trifle!

ROXANE [warmly].
Did he doubt
Of what I said?--Ah, yes, I saw he doubted!

CYRANO [taking her hand].
But are you sure you told him all the truth?

ROXANE.

Yes, I would love him were he. . .

[She hesitates.]

CYRANO.
Does that word
Embarrass you before my face, Roxane?

ROXANE.
I. . .

CYRANO [smiling sadly].
'Twill not hurt me! Say it! If he were
Ugly!. . .

ROXANE.
Yes, ugly!
[Musket report outside]
Hark! I hear a shot!

CYRANO [ardently].
Hideous!

ROXANE.
Hideous! yes!

CYRANO.
Disfigured.

ROXANE.
Ay!

CYRANO.
Grotesque?

ROXANE.

He could not be grotesque to me!

CYRANO.
You'd love the same?. . .

ROXANE.
The same--nay, even more!

CYRANO [losing command over himself--aside].
My God! it's true, perchance, love waits me there!
[To Roxane]
I. . .Roxane. . .listen. . .

LE BRET [entering hurriedly--to Cyrano].
Cyrano!

CYRANO [turning round].
What?

LE BRET.
Hush!

[He whispers something to him.]

CYRANO [letting go Roxane's hand and exclaiming].
Ah, God!

ROXANE.
What is it?

CYRANO [to himself--stunned].
All is over now.

[Renewed reports.]

ROXANE.

What is the matter? Hark! another shot!

[She goes up to look outside.]

CYRANO.
It is too late, now I can never tell!

ROXANE [trying to rush out].
What has chanced?

CYRANO [rushing to stop her].
Nothing!

[Some cadets enter, trying to hide something they are carrying, and
close round it to prevent Roxane approaching.]

ROXANE.
And those men?
[Cyrano draws her away.]
What were you just about to say before. . .?

CYRANO.
What was I saying? Nothing now, I swear!
[Solemnly]
I swear that Christian's soul, his nature, were. . .
[Hastily correcting himself]
Nay, that they are, the noblest, greatest. . .

ROXANE.
Were?
[With a loud scream]
Oh!

[She rushes up, pushing every one aside.]

CYRANO.

All is over now!

ROXANE [seeing Christian lying on the ground, wrapped in his cloak]
O Christian!

LE BRET [to Cyrano].
Struck by first shot of the enemy!

[Roxane flings herself down by Christian. Fresh reports of cannon--
        clash of arms--clamor--beating of drums.]

CARBON [with sword in the air].
O come! Your muskets.

[Followed by the cadets, he passes to the other side of the ramparts.]

ROXANE.
Christian!

THE VOICE OF CARBON [from the other side].
Ho! make haste!

ROXANE.
Christian!

CARBON.
FORM LINE!

ROXANE.
Christian!

CARBON.
HANDLE YOUR MATCH!

[Ragueneau rushes up, bringing water in a helmet.]

CHRISTIAN [in a dying voice].
Roxane!

CYRANO [quickly, whispering into Christian's ear, while Roxane
distractedly tears a piece of linen from his breast, which she dips into
the water, trying to stanch the bleeding].
I told her all. She loves you still.

[Christian closes his eyes.]

ROXANE.
How, my sweet love?

CARBON.
DRAW RAMRODS!

ROXANE [to Cyrano].
He is not dead?

CARBON.
OPEN YOUR CHARGES WITH YOUR TEETH!

ROXANE.
His cheek
Grows cold against my own!

CARBON.
READY! PRESENT!

ROXANE [seeing a letter in Christian's doublet].
A letter!. . .
'Tis for me!

[She opens it.]

CYRANO [aside].

My letter!

CARBON.
FIRE!

[Musket reports--shouts--noise of battle.]

CYRANO [trying to disengage his hand, which Roxane on her knees is holding].
But, Roxane, hark, they fight!

ROXANE [detaining him].
Stay yet awhile.
For he is dead. You knew him, you alone.
[Weeping quietly]
Ah, was not his a beauteous soul, a soul
Wondrous!

CYRANO [standing up--bareheaded].
Ay, Roxane.

ROXANE.
An inspired poet?

CYRANO.
Ay, Roxane.

ROXANE.
And a mind sublime?

CYRANO.
Oh, yes!

ROXANE.
A heart too deep for common minds to plumb,
A spirit subtle, charming?

CYRANO [firmly].
Ay, Roxane.

ROXANE [flinging herself on the dead body].
Dead, my love!

CYRANO [aside--drawing his sword].
Ay, and let me die to-day,
Since, all unconscious, she mourns me--in him!

[Sounds of trumpets in the distance.]

DE GUICHE [appearing on the ramparts--bareheaded--with a wound
on his forehead--in a voice of thunder].
It is the signal! Trumpet flourishes!
The French bring the provisions into camp!
Hold but the place awhile!

ROXANE.
See, there is blood
Upon the letter--tears!

A VOICE [outside--shouting].
Surrender!

VOICE OF CADETS.
No!

RAGUENEAU [standing on the top of his carriage, watches the battle
over the edge of the ramparts].
The danger's ever greater!

CYRANO [to De Guiche--pointing to Roxane].
I will charge!
Take her away!

ROXANE [kissing the letter--in a half-extinguished voice].
O God! his tears! his blood!. . .

RAGUENEAU [jumping down from the carriage and rushing
toward her].
She's swooned away!

DE GUICHE [on the rampart--to the cadets--with fury].
Stand fast!

A VOICE [outside].
Lay down your arms!

THE CADETS.
No!

CYRANO [to De Guiche].
Now that you have proved your valor, Sir,
[Pointing to Roxane]
Fly, and save her!

DE GUICHE [rushing to Roxane, and carrying her away in his arms].
So be it! Gain but time,
The victory's ours!

CYRANO.
Good.
[Calling out to Roxane, whom De Guiche, aided by Ragueneau, is
bearing away in a fainting condition]
Farewell, Roxane!

[Tumult. Shouts. Cadets reappear, wounded, falling on the scene.
Cyrano, rushing to the battle, is stopped by Carbon de Castel-Jaloux,
who is streaming with blood.]

CARBON.

We are breaking! I am wounded--wounded twice!

CYRANO [shouting to the Gascons].
GASCONS! HO, GASCONS! NEVER TURN YOUR BACKS!
[To Carbon, whom he is supporting]
Have no fear! I have two deaths to avenge:
My friend who's slain;--and my dead happiness!
[They come down, Cyrano brandishing the lance to which is attached
Roxane's handkerchief.]
Float there! laced kerchief broidered with her name!
[He sticks it in the ground and shouts to the cadets.]
FALL ON THEM, GASCONS! CRUSH THEM!
[To the fifer]
Fifer, play!

[The fife plays. The wounded try to rise. Some cadets, falling one over
the other down the slope, group themselves round Cyrano and the
little flag. The carriage is crowded with men inside and outside, and,
bristling with arquebuses, is turned into a fortress.]

A CADET [appearing on the crest, beaten backward, but still fighting,
cries].
They're climbing the redoubt!
[and falls dead.]

CYRANO.
Let us salute them!
[The rampart is covered instantly by a formidable row of enemies. The
standards of the Imperialists are raised.]
Fire!

[General discharge.]

A CRY IN THE ENEMY'S RANKS.
Fire!

[A deadly answering volley. The cadets fall on all sides.]

A SPANISH OFFICER [uncovering].
Who are these men who rush on death?

CYRANO [reciting, erect, amid a storm of bullets].
The bold Cadets of Gascony,
Of Carbon of Castel-Jaloux!
Brawling, swaggering boastfully,
[He rushes forward, followed by a few survivors.]
The bold Cadets. . .

[His voice is drowned in the battle.]

[Curtain.]

ACT V

Cyrano's Gazette.

Fifteen years later, in 1655. Park of the Sisters of the Holy Cross in Paris. Magnificent trees. On the left the house: broad steps on to which open several doors. An enormous plane tree in the middle of the stage, standing alone. On the right, among big boxwood trees, a semi-circular stone bench.

The whole background of the stage is crossed by an alley of chestnut trees leading on the right hand to the door of a chapel seen through the branches. Through the double row of trees of this alley are seen lawns, other alleys, clusters of trees, winding of the park, the sky.

The chapel opens by a little side door on to a colonnade which is wreathed with autumn leaves, and is lost to view a little farther on in the right-hand foreground behind the boxwood.

It is autumn. All the foliage is red against the fresh green of the lawns. The green boxwood and yews stand out dark.

Under each tree a patch of yellow leaves.

The stage is strewn with dead leaves, which rustle under foot in the alleys, and half cover the steps and benches.

Between the benches on the right hand and the tree a large embroidery frame, in front of which a little chair has been set.

Baskets full of skeins and balls of wool. A tapestry begun.

At the rising of the curtains nuns are walking to and fro in the park; some are seated on the bench around an older Sister.

The leaves are falling.

Act V. Scene I.

[Mother Marguerite, Sister Martha, Sister Claire, other sisters.]

SISTER MARTHA [to Mother Marguerite].
Sister Claire glanced in the mirror, once--nay, twice, to see if her coif suited.

MOTHER MARGUERITE [to Sister Claire].
'Tis not well.

SISTER CLAIRE.
But I saw Sister Martha take a plum
Out of the tart.

MOTHER MARGUERITE [to Sister Martha].
That was ill done, my sister.

SISTER CLAIRE.
A little glance!

SISTER MARTHA.
And such a little plum!

MOTHER MARGUERITE.
I shall tell this to Monsieur Cyrano.

SISTER CLAIRE.
Nay, prithee do not!--he will mock!

SISTER MARTHA.
He'll say we nuns are vain!

SISTER CLAIRE.
And greedy!

MOTHER MARGUERITE [smiling].
Ay, and kind!

SISTER CLAIRE.
Is it not true, pray, Mother Marguerite,
That he has come, each week, on Saturday
For ten years, to the convent?

MOTHER MARGUERITE.
Ay! and more!
Ever since--fourteen years ago--the day
His cousin brought here, 'midst our woolen coifs,
The worldly mourning of her widow's veil,
Like a blackbird's wing among the convent doves!

SISTER MARTHA.
He only has the skill to turn her mind
From grief--unsoftened yet by Time--unhealed!

ALL THE SISTERS.
He is so droll!--It's cheerful when he comes!--

He teases us!--But we all like him well!--
--We make him pasties of angelica!

SISTER MARTHA.
But, he is not a faithful Catholic!

SISTER CLAIRE.
We will convert him!

THE SISTERS.
Yes! Yes!

MOTHER MARGUERITE.
I forbid,
My daughters, you attempt that subject. Nay,
Weary him not--he might less oft come here!

SISTER MARTHA.
But. . .God. . .

MOTHER MARGUERITE.
Nay, never fear! God knows him well!

SISTER MARTHA.
But--every Saturday, when he arrives,
He tells me, 'Sister, I eat meat on Friday!'

MOTHER MARGUERITE.
Ah! says he so? Well, the last time he came
Food had not passed his lips for two whole days!

SISTER MARTHA.
Mother!

MOTHER MARGUERITE.
He's poor.

SISTER MARTHA.
Who told you so, dear Mother?

MOTHER MARGUERITE.
Monsieur Le Bret.

SISTER MARTHA.
None help him?

MOTHER MARGUERITE.
He permits not.
[In an alley at the back Roxane appears, dressed in black, with a widow's coif and veil. De Guiche, imposing-looking and visibly aged, walks by her side. They saunter slowly. Mother Marguerite rises.]
'Tis time we go in; Madame Madeleine
Walks in the garden with a visitor.

SISTER MARTHA [to Sister Claire, in a low voice].
The Marshal of Grammont?

SISTER CLAIRE [looking at him].
'Tis he, I think.

SISTER MARTHA.
'Tis many months now since he came to see her.

THE SISTERS.
He is so busy!--The Court,--the camp!. . .

SISTER CLAIRE.
The world!

[They go out. De Guiche and Roxane come forward in silence, and stop close to the embroidery frame.]

Act V. Scene II.

[Roxane; the Duke de Grammont, formerly Count de Guiche. Then
Le Bret and Ragueneau.]

THE DUKE.
And you stay here still--ever vainly fair,
Ever in weeds?

ROXANE.
Ever.

THE DUKE.
Still faithful?

ROXANE.
Still.

THE DUKE [after a pause].
Am I forgiven?

ROXANE.
Ay, since I am here.

[Another pause.]

THE DUKE.
His was a soul, you say?. . .

ROXANE.
Ah!--when you knew him!

THE DUKE.
Ah, may be!. . .I, perchance, too little knew him!
. . .And his last letter, ever next your heart?

ROXANE.
Hung from this chain, a gentle scapulary.

THE DUKE.
And, dead, you love him still?

ROXANE.
At times,--meseems
He is but partly dead--our hearts still speak,
As if his love, still living, wrapped me round!

THE DUKE [after another pause].
Cyrano comes to see you?

ROXANE.
Often, ay.
Dear, kind old friend! We call him my 'Gazette.'
He never fails to come: beneath this tree
They place his chair, if it be fine:--I wait,
I broider;--the clock strikes;--at the last stroke
I hear,--for now I never turn to look--
Too sure to hear his cane tap down the steps;
He seats himself:--with gentle raillery
He mocks my tapestry that's never done;
He tells me all the gossip of the week. . .
[Le Bret appears on the steps.]
Why, here's Le Bret!
[Le Bret descends.]
How goes it with our friend?

LE BRET.
Ill!--very ill.

THE DUKE.
How?

ROXANE [to the Duke].
He exaggerates!

LE BRET.

All that I prophesied: desertion, want!. . .
His letters now make him fresh enemies!--
Attacking the sham nobles, sham devout,
Sham brave,--the thieving authors,--all the world!

ROXANE.

Ah! but his sword still holds them all in check;
None get the better of him.

THE DUKE [shaking his head].
Time will show!

LE BRET.

Ah, but I fear for him--not man's attack,--
Solitude--hunger--cold December days,
That wolf-like steal into his chamber drear:--
Lo! the assassins that I fear for him!
Each day he tightens by one hole his belt:
That poor nose--tinted like old ivory:
He has retained one shabby suit of serge.

THE DUKE.

Ay, there is one who has no prize of Fortune!--
Yet is not to be pitied!

LE BRET [with a bitter smile].
My Lord Marshal!. . .

THE DUKE.

Pity him not! He has lived out his vows,
Free in his thoughts, as in his actions free!

LE BRET [in the same tone].
My Lord!. . .

THE DUKE [haughtily].
True! I have all, and he has naught;. . .
Yet I were proud to take his hand!
[Bowing to Roxane]
Adieu!

ROXANE.
I go with you.

[The Duke bows to Le Bret, and goes with Roxane toward the steps.]

THE DUKE [pausing, while she goes up].
Ay, true,--I envy him.
Look you, when life is brimful of success
--Though the past hold no action foul--one feels
A thousand self-disgusts, of which the sum
Is not remorse, but a dim, vague unrest;
And, as one mounts the steps of worldly fame,
The Duke's furred mantles trail within their folds
A sound of dead illusions, vain regrets,
A rustle--scarce a whisper--like as when,
Mounting the terrace steps, by your mourning robe
Sweeps in its train the dying autumn leaves.

ROXANE [ironically].
You are pensive?

THE DUKE.
True! I am!
[As he is going out, suddenly]
Monsieur Le Bret!
[To Roxane]
A word, with your permission?
[He goes to Le Bret, and in a low voice]
True, that none
Dare to attack your friend;--but many hate him;

Yesterday, at the Queen's card-play, 'twas said
'That Cyrano may die--by accident!'
Let him stay in--be prudent!

LE BRET [raising his arms to heaven].
Prudent! He!. . .
He's coming here. I'll warn him--but!. . .

ROXANE [who has stayed on the steps, to a sister who comes
toward her].
What is it?

THE SISTER.
Ragueneau would see you, Madame.

ROXANE.
Let him come.
[To the Duke and Le Bret]
He comes to tell his troubles. Having been
An author (save the mark!)--poor fellow--now
By turns he's singer. . .

LE BRET.
Bathing-man. . .

ROXANE.
Then actor. . .

LE BRET.
Beadle. . .

ROXANE.
Wig-maker. . .

LE BRET.
Teacher of the lute. . .

ROXANE.
What will he be to-day, by chance?

RAGUENEAU [entering hurriedly].
Ah! Madame!
[He sees Le Bret.]
Ah! you here, Sir!

ROXANE [smiling].
Tell all your miseries
To him; I will return anon.

RAGUENEAU.
But, Madame. . .

[Roxane goes out with the Duke. Ragueneau goes toward Le Bret.]

Act V. Scene III.

[Le Bret, Ragueneau.]

RAGUENEAU.
Since you are here, 'tis best she should not know!
I was going to your friend just now--was but
A few steps from the house, when I saw him
Go out. I hurried to him. Saw him turn
The corner. . .suddenly, from out a window
Where he was passing--was it chance?. . .may be!
A lackey let fall a large piece of wood.

LE BRET.
Cowards! O Cyrano!

RAGUENEAU.
I ran--I saw. . .

LE BRET.
'Tis hideous!

RAGUENEAU.
Saw our poet, Sir--our friend--
Struck to the ground--a large wound in his head!

LE BRET.
He's dead?

RAGUENEAU.
No--but--I bore him to his room. . .
Ah! his room! What a thing to see!--that garret!

LE BRET.
He suffers?

RAGUENEAU.
No, his consciousness has flown.

LE BRET.
Saw you a doctor?

RAGUENEAU.
One was kind--he came.

LE BRET.
My poor Cyrano!--We must not tell this
To Roxane suddenly.--What said this leech?--

RAGUENEAU.
Said,--what, I know not--fever, meningitis!--
Ah! could you see him--all his head bound up!--
But let us haste!--There's no one by his bed!--
And if he try to rise, Sir, he might die!

LE BRET [dragging him toward the right].
Come! Through the chapel! 'Tis the quickest way!

ROXANE [appearing on the steps, and seeing Le Bret go away by the colonnade leading to the chapel door].
Monsieur le Bret!
[Le Bret and Ragueneau disappear without answering.]
Le Bret goes--when I call!
'Tis some new trouble of good Ragueneau's.

[She descends the steps.]

Act V. Scene IV.

[Roxane alone. Two sisters, for a moment.]

ROXANE.
Ah! what a beauty in September's close!
My sorrow's eased. April's joy dazzled it,
But autumn wins it with her dying calm.
[She seats herself at the embroidery frame. Two sisters come out of the house, and bring a large armchair under the tree.]
There comes the famous armchair where he sits,
Dear faithful friend!

SISTER MARTHA.
It is the parlor's best!

ROXANE.
Thanks, sister.
[The sisters go.]
He'll be here now.
[She seats herself. A clock strikes.]
The hour strikes.
--My silks?--Why, now, the hour's struck!
How strange

To be behind his time, at last, to-day!
Perhaps the portress--where's my thimble?. . .
Here!--Is preaching to him.
[A pause]
Yes, she must be preaching!
Surely he must come soon!--Ah, a dead leaf!--
[She brushes off the leaf from her work.]
Nothing, besides, could--scissors?--In my bag!
--Could hinder him. . .

A SISTER [coming to the steps].
Monsieur de Bergerac.

Act V. Scene V.

[Roxane, Cyrano and, for a moment, Sister Martha.]

ROXANE [without turning round].
What was I saying?. . .
[She embroiders. Cyrano, very pale, his hat pulled down over his eyes,
appears. The sister who had announced him retires. He descends the
steps slowly, with a visible difficulty in holding himself upright, bearing
heavily on his cane. Roxane still works at her tapestry.]
Time has dimmed the tints. . .
How harmonize them now?
[To Cyrano, with playful reproach]
For the first time
Late!--For the first time, all these fourteen years!

CYRANO [who has succeeded in reaching the chair, and has seated
himself--in a lively voice, which is in great contrast with his pale face].
Ay! It is villainous! I raged--was stayed. . .

ROXANE.
By?. . .

CYRANO.
By a bold, unwelcome visitor.

ROXANE [absently, working].
Some creditor?

CYRANO.
Ay, cousin,--the last creditor
Who has a debt to claim from me.

ROXANE.
And you
Have paid it?

CYRANO.
No, not yet! I put it off;
--Said, 'Cry you mercy; this is Saturday,
When I have get a standing rendezvous
That naught defers. Call in an hour's time!'

ROXANE [carelessly].
Oh, well, a creditor can always wait!
I shall not let you go ere twilight falls.

CYRANO.
Haply, perforce, I quit you ere it falls!

[He shuts his eyes, and is silent for a moment. Sister Martha crosses
the park from the chapel to the flight of steps. Roxane, seeing her,
signs to her to approach.]

ROXANE [to Cyrano].
How now? You have not teased the Sister?

CYRANO [hastily opening his eyes].
True!

[In a comically loud voice]
Sister! come here!
[The sister glides up to him.]
Ha! ha! What? Those bright eyes
Bent ever on the ground?

SISTER MARTHA [who makes a movement of astonishment on
seeing his face].
Oh!

CYRANO [in a whisper, pointing to Roxane].
Hush! 'tis naught!--
[Loudly, in a blustering voice]
I broke fast yesterday!

SISTER MARTHA [aside].
I know, I know!
That's how he is so pale! Come presently
To the refectory, I'll make you drink
A famous bowl of soup. . .You'll come?

CYRANO.
Ay, ay!

SISTER MARTHA.
There, see! You are more reasonable to-day!

ROXANE [who hears them whispering].
The Sister would convert you?

SISTER MARTHA.
Nay, not I!

CYRANO.
Hold! but it's true! You preach to me no more,
You, once so glib with holy words! I am

Astonished!. . .

[With burlesque fury]

Stay, I will surprise you too!

Hark! I permit you. . .

[He pretends to be seeking for something to tease her with, and to
have found it.]

. . .It is something new!--

To--pray for me, to-night, at chapel-time!

ROXANE.
Oh! oh!

CYRANO [laughing].
Good Sister Martha is struck dumb!

SISTER MARTHA [gently].
I did not wait your leave to pray for you.

[She goes out.]

CYRANO [turning to Roxane, who is still bending over her work].
That tapestry! Beshrew me if my eyes
Will ever see it finished!

ROXANE.
I was sure
To hear that well-known jest!

[A light breeze causes the leaves to fall.]

CYRANO.
The autumn leaves!

ROXANE [lifting her head, and looking down the distant alley].
Soft golden brown, like a Venetian's hair.
--See how they fall!

CYRANO.
Ay, see how brave they fall,
In their last journey downward from the bough,
To rot within the clay; yet, lovely still,
Hiding the horror of the last decay,
With all the wayward grace of careless flight!

ROXANE.
What, melancholy--you?

CYRANO [collecting himself].
Nay, nay, Roxane!

ROXANE.
Then let the dead leaves fall the way they will. . .
And chat. What, have you nothing new to tell,
My Court Gazette?

CYRANO.
Listen.

ROXANE.
Ah!

CYRANO [growing whiter and whiter].
Saturday
The nineteenth: having eaten to excess
Of pear-conserve, the King felt feverish;
The lancet quelled this treasonable revolt,
And the august pulse beats at normal pace.
At the Queen's ball on Sunday thirty score
Of best white waxen tapers were consumed.
Our troops, they say, have chased the Austrians.
Four sorcerers were hanged. The little dog
Of Madame d'Athis took a dose. . .

ROXANE.
I bid
You hold your tongue, Monsieur de Bergerac!

CYRANO.
Monday--not much--Claire changed protector.

ROXANE.
Oh!

CYRANO [whose face changes more and more].
Tuesday, the Court repaired to Fontainebleau.
Wednesday, the Montglat said to Comte de Fiesque. . .
No! Thursday--Mancini, Queen of France! (almost!)
Friday, the Monglat to Count Fiesque said--'Yes!'
And Saturday the twenty-sixth. . .

[He closes his eyes. His head falls forward. Silence.]

ROXANE [surprised at his voice ceasing, turns round, looks at him,
and rising, terrified].
He swoons!
[She runs toward him crying.]
Cyrano!

CYRANO [opening his eyes, in an unconcerned voice].
What is this?
[He sees Roxane bending over him, and, hastily pressing his hat on his
head, and shrinking back in his chair.]
Nay, on my word
'Tis nothing! Let me be!

ROXANE.
But. . .

CYRANO.

That old wound
Of Arras, sometimes,--as you know. . .

ROXANE.
Dear friend!

CYRANO.
'Tis nothing, 'twill pass soon;
[He smiles with an effort.]
See!--it has passed!

ROXANE.
Each of us has his wound; ay, I have mine,--
Never healed up--not healed yet, my old wound!
[She puts her hand on her breast.]
'Tis here, beneath this letter brown with age,
All stained with tear-drops, and still stained with blood.

[Twilight begins to fall.]

CYRANO.
His letter! Ah! you promised me one day
That I should read it.

ROXANE.
What would you?--His letter?

CYRANO.
Yes, I would fain,--to-day. . .

ROXANE [giving the bag hung at her neck].
See! here it is!

CYRANO [taking it].
Have I your leave to open?

ROXANE.
Open--read!

[She comes back to her tapestry frame, folds it up, sorts her wools.]

CYRANO [reading].
'Roxane, adieu! I soon must die!
This very night, beloved; and I
Feel my soul heavy with love untold.
I die! No more, as in days of old,
My loving, longing eyes will feast
On your least gesture--ay, the least!
I mind me the way you touch your cheek
With your finger, softly, as you speak!
Ah me! I know that gesture well!
My heart cries out!--I cry "Farewell"!'

ROXANE.
But how you read that letter! One would think. . .

CYRANO [continuing to read].
'My life, my love, my jewel, my sweet,
My heart has been yours in every beat!'

[The shades of evening fall imperceptibly.]

ROXANE.
You read in such a voice--so strange--and yet--
It is not the first time I hear that voice!

[She comes nearer very softly, without his perceiving it, passes behind
his chair, and, noiselessly leaning over him, looks at the letter. The
darkness deepens.]

CYRANO.
'Here, dying, and there, in the land on high,

I am he who loved, who loves you,--I. . .'

ROXANE [putting her hand on his shoulder].
How can you read? It is too dark to see!
[He starts, turns, sees her close to him. Suddenly alarmed, he holds his
head down. Then in the dusk, which has now completely enfolded
them, she says, very slowly, with clasped hands.]
And, fourteen years long, he has played this part
Of the kind old friend who comes to laugh and chat.

CYRANO.
Roxane!

ROXANE.
'Twas you!

CYRANO.
No, never; Roxane, no!

ROXANE.
I should have guessed, each time he said my name!

CYRANO.
No, it was not I!

ROXANE.
It was you!

CYRANO.
I swear!

ROXANE.
I see through all the generous counterfeit--
The letters--you!

CYRANO.

No.

ROXANE.
The sweet, mad love-words!
You!

CYRANO.
No!

ROXANE.
The voice that thrilled the night--you, you!

CYRANO.
I swear you err.

ROXANE.
The soul--it was your soul!

CYRANO.
I loved you not.

ROXANE.
You loved me not?

CYRANO.
'Twas he!

ROXANE.
You loved me!

CYRANO.
No!

ROXANE.
See! how you falter now!

CYRANO.
No, my sweet love, I never loved you!

ROXANE.
Ah!
Things dead, long dead, see! how they rise again!
--Why, why keep silence all these fourteen years,
When, on this letter, which he never wrote,
The tears were your tears?

CYRANO [holding out the letter to her].
The bloodstains were his.

ROXANE.
Why, then, that noble silence,--kept so long--
Broken to-day for the first time--why?

CYRANO.
Why?. . .

[Le Bret and Ragueneau enter running.]

Act V. Scene VI.

[The same. Le Bret and Ragueneau.]

LE BRET.
What madness! Here? I knew it well!

CYRANO [smiling and sitting up].
What now?

LE BRET.
He has brought his death by coming, Madame.

ROXANE.

God!
Ah, then! that faintness of a moment since. . .?

CYRANO.
Why, true! It interrupted the 'Gazette:'
. . .Saturday, twenty-sixth, at dinner-time,
Assassination of De Bergerac.

[He takes off his hat; they see his head bandaged.]

ROXANE.
What says he? Cyrano!--His head all bound!
Ah, what has chanced? How?--Who?. . .

CYRANO.
'To be struck down,
Pierced by sword i' the heart, from a hero's hand!'
That I had dreamed. O mockery of Fate!
--Killed, I! of all men--in an ambuscade!
Struck from behind, and by a lackey's hand!
'Tis very well. I am foiled, foiled in all,
Even in my death.

RAGUENEAU.
Ah, Monsieur!. . .

CYRANO [holding out his hand to him].
Ragueneau,
Weep not so bitterly!. . .What do you now,
Old comrade?

RAGUENEAU [amid his tears].
Trim the lights for Moliere's stage.

CYRANO.
Moliere!

RAGUENEAU.
Yes; but I shall leave to-morrow.
I cannot bear it!--Yesterday, they played
'Scapin'--I saw he'd thieved a scene from you!

LE BRET.
What! a whole scene?

RAGUENEAU.
Oh, yes, indeed, Monsieur,
The famous one, 'Que Diable allait-il faire?'

LE BRET.
Moliere has stolen that?

CYRANO.
Tut! He did well!. . .
[To Ragueneau].
How went the scene? It told--I think it told?

RAGUENEAU [sobbing].
Ah! how they laughed!

CYRANO.
Look you, it was my life
To be the prompter every one forgets!
[To Roxane].
That night when 'neath your window Christian spoke
--Under your balcony, you remember? Well!
There was the allegory of my whole life:
I, in the shadow, at the ladder's foot,
While others lightly mount to Love and Fame!
Just! very just! Here on the threshold drear
Of death, I pay my tribute with the rest,
To Moliere's genius,--Christian's fair face!
[The chapel-bell chimes. The nuns are seen passing down the alley at

the back, to say their office.]
Let them go pray, go pray, when the bell rings!

ROXANE [rising and calling].
Sister! Sister!

CYRANO [holding her fast].
Call no one. Leave me not;
When you come back, I should be gone for aye.
[The nuns have all entered the chapel. The organ sounds.]
I was somewhat fain for music—hark! 'tis come.

ROXANE.
Live, for I love you!

CYRANO.
No, In fairy tales
When to the ill-starred Prince the lady says
'I love you!' all his ugliness fades fast—
But I remain the same, up to the last!

ROXANE.
I have marred your life—I, I!

CYRANO.
You blessed my life!
Never on me had rested woman's love.
My mother even could not find me fair:
I had no sister; and, when grown a man,
I feared the mistress who would mock at me.
But I have had your friendship—grace to you
A woman's charm has passed across my path.

LE BRET [pointing to the moon, which is seen between the trees].
Your other lady-love is come.

CYRANO [smiling].
I see.

ROXANE.
I loved but once, yet twice I lose my love!

CYRANO.
Hark you, Le Bret! I soon shall reach the moon.
To-night, alone, with no projectile's aid!. . .

LE BRET.
What are you saying?

CYRANO.
I tell you, it is there,
There, that they send me for my Paradise,
There I shall find at last the souls I love,
In exile,--Galileo--Socrates!

LE BRET [rebelliously].
No, no! It is too clumsy, too unjust!
So great a heart! So great a poet! Die
Like this? what, die. . .?

CYRANO.
Hark to Le Bret, who scolds!

LE BRET [weeping].
Dear friend. . .

CYRANO [starting up, his eyes wild].
What ho! Cadets of Gascony!
The elemental mass--ah yes! The hic. . .

LE BRET.
His science still--he raves!

CYRANO.
Copernicus
Said. . .

ROXANE.
Oh!

CYRANO.
Mais que diable allait-il faire,
Mais que diable allait-il faire dans cette galere?. . .
Philosopher, metaphysician,
Rhymer, brawler, and musician,
Famed for his lunar expedition,
And the unnumbered duels he fought,--
And lover also,--by interposition!--
Here lies Hercule Savinien
De Cyrano de Bergerac,
Who was everything, yet was naught.
I cry you pardon, but I may not stay;
See, the moon-ray that comes to call me hence!
[He has fallen back in his chair; the sobs of Roxane recall him to real-
ity; he looks long at her, and, touching her veil]
I would not bid you mourn less faithfully
That good, brave Christian: I would only ask
That when my body shall be cold in clay
You wear those sable mourning weeds for two,
And mourn awhile for me, in mourning him.

ROXANE.
I swear it you!. . .

CYRANO [shivering violently, then suddenly rising].
Not there! what, seated?--no!
[They spring toward him.]
Let no one hold me up--
[He props himself against the tree.]

Only the tree!
[Silence]
It comes. E'en now my feet have turned to stone,
My hands are gloved with lead!
[He stands erect.]
But since Death comes,
I meet him still afoot,
[He draws his sword.]
And sword in hand!

LE BRET.
Cyrano!

ROXANE [half fainting].
Cyrano!

[All shrink back in terror.]

CYRANO.
Why, I well believe
He dares to mock my nose? Ho! insolent!
[He raises his sword.]
What say you? It is useless? Ay, I know
But who fights ever hoping for success?
I fought for lost cause, and for fruitless quest!
You there, who are you!--You are thousands!
Ah!
I know you now, old enemies of mine!
Falsehood!
[He strikes in air with his sword.]
Have at you! Ha! and Compromise!
Prejudice, Treachery!. . .
[He strikes.]
Surrender, I?
Parley? No, never! You too, Folly,--you?
I know that you will lay me low at last;

Let be! Yet I fall fighting, fighting still!
[He makes passes in the air, and stops, breathless.]
You strip from me the laurel and the rose!
Take all! Despite you there is yet one thing
I hold against you all, and when, to-night,
I enter Christ's fair courts, and, lowly bowed,
Sweep with doffed casque the heavens' threshold blue,
One thing is left, that, void of stain or smutch,
I bear away despite you.

[He springs forward, his sword raised; it falls from his hand; he
staggers, falls back into the arms of Le Bret and Ragueneau.]

ROXANE [bending and kissing his forehead].
'Tis?. . .

CYRANO [opening his eyes, recognizing her, and smiling].
MY PANACHE.

[Curtain.]

THE END

DISCUSSION QUESTIONS

1. What does the playwright, Edmond Rostand, accomplish with the chaotic opening scene?
2. Why do you think the presence of the play's protagonist, Cyrano de Bergerac, is delayed despite the other characters referencing and talking about him repeatedly prior to his appearance?
3. What does Cyrano's exceedingly large nose symbolize?
4. How does Cyrano's exceptional wit and use of poetry distinguish him from other characters?
5. Why does Cyrano so despise Montfleury, and what does this rivalry reveal about Cyrano's insecurities?
6. How does Ragueneau's fondness for poetry and the subsequent obstacles he faces foreshadow Cyrano's own predicament?
7. What does Roxane's fixation with one's ability to speak eloquently and poetically represent?
8. How are Cyrano and Christian literary foils?
9. How does the constant threat of violence and war impact the various characters, and what does it reveal about their differing motivations?

10. In what ways is Roxane manipulative and persuasive? In what ways does she take advantage of her suitors' adoration?

11. Does Christian's inability to poetically articulate his feelings for Roxanne make his affection for her any less true or valid?

12. How does De Guiche compare to Cyrano, and what does his villainous persona symbolize?

13. How does the source of the play's humor in Acts I and II shift in Act III?

14. How does the war with the Spaniards mirror the romantic conflict of the play?

15. In what ways does De Guiche redeem himself, transforming from a villain to a hero? Is he successful?

16. How does Cyrano maintain his honor and integrity despite his duplicity?

17. In Act V, what does the combination of Cyrano's tears and Christian's blood, smeared upon Christian/Cyrano's final letter to Roxane, symbolize?

18. What is the significance regarding the way in which Cyrano dies—from a falling log hitting his head as opposed to heroically in battle?

19. What themes are explored throughout this play?

20. Why is *Cyrano de Bergerac* classified as a heroic comedy? What differentiates it from other comedic genres, and what role does comedy serve throughout the play? Would a different genre classification be more fitting?

Portrait of Edmond Rostand

Made in the USA
Monee, IL
29 June 2021